Praise for *Changing*

"This book is a must read for all female entrepreneurs. As a previous corporate strategist and current founder and CEO of my own company, I live by the words "knowledge is power." This book provides just that. Jenn does a beautiful job of providing transparency and clarity with the necessary how-to's for navigating the waters ahead."
— Maria Malavenda, Founder, EVVEMI

"As an angel investor, I've focused on women-led companies because they have been historically underfunded yet have delivered above-market returns. *Changing Tides* provides insight and inspiration for both female founders and the smart investors who invest in them."
— Nancy Hayes, Angel Investor

"As one who works with female founders around the world, it's refreshing to see how well this book illustrates the extent to which both opportunities and challenges are shared globally. *Changing Tides* goes beyond storytelling, catalyzing collaborative, innovative solutions towards meaningful progress for female founders, for women, for society."
—Lucie Newcomb, Founder & CEO/CMO,
The NewComm Global Group

"Numbers don't lie. As an investor, I seek better returns. *Changing Tides* makes a clear and data-driven business case for investing in female founders. All investors should read this book."
— Zeynep Urgun Zorlu, Global Investor, Zurgun Capital

"*Changing Tides* is exactly what every female founder — and every investor — needs. It's a rallying cry for all of us who support female founders. A peek into what the collective experience is, and what is needed to lift up and propel these founders and create better, more diverse offerings in this world."
—Ari Horie, Founder, Women's Startup Lab

A Curated Essay Collection by
JENNIFER S. LEBLANC

changing
tides

Powerful Strategies for
Female Founders

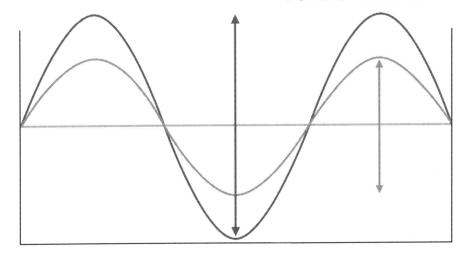

Changing Tides: Powerful Strategies for Female Founders
Published by
HAL House

HH

HAL HOUSE

Editor: Kay Paumier
Cover design: Gabriela Martinez
Book design: Laura Boyle
Production assistant: Olivia Dippon

ISBN (paperback edition): 978-1-7321639-6-6
ISBN (e-book edition): 978-1-7321639-8-0

Printed in the United States of America

**Dedicated to all the female founders and funders
who are working to change the tides**

A portion of the proceeds from this book will be donated to All Raise,
a nonprofit organization dedicated to diversity in funders and founders.

"Never give up, for that is just the place and time
that the tide will turn."

— Harriet Beecher Stowe

Acknowledgements

THIS BOOK CAME out of the blue for me in the summer of 2017, when the sexual harassment cases of Justin Caldbeck (Silicon Valley venture capitalist) and Dave McClure (500 Startups) were greeted with deafening silence by Silicon Valley. The normally chattering social media was strangely quiet. This was before the #MeToo movement.

I knew from my experience in Silicon Valley and the stories I'd heard from other women that the Valley was an "unequal opportunity zone." After the sexual harassment stories came out, I knew something had to be done to change the culture. I just didn't know I would be involved.

I discussed my concern—and yes, my outrage—about the way that female founders were treated in Silicon Valley with my coach, Don Ramer. I insisted that someone who knew about the female founder experience should do something. I said that this person should be familiar with the work some female investors were doing to change the culture in Silicon Valley. After several heated discussions, Don convinced me that I was the person to shine the light on the challenges female founders face. He convinced me that I needed to undertake *Changing Tides*. Don, you were absolutely right.

Over the course of the year, this book has led me to many interesting conversations and collaborations with the contributors. These amazing people generously share their stories, experiences and words of wisdom in these pages. I am deeply grateful to each of them for joining me on this journey to change the tides. *Thank you, Amy Belt Raimundo, Tammy Bowers, Suzanne Fletcher, Maha Ibrahim, Deb Kilpatrick, Xandra Laskowski, Jessica Livingston, Terri (Hanson) Mead, Mukund Mohan, Gillian Muessig, Kate Purmal, Dorin Rosenshine, Debra Vernon and Robyn Ward.*

Most of all, I want to thank my family for supporting me in this second book project the same year my first book was published. It was a herculean undertaking, but we did it. Thanks to my husband, David Hedley, who bore the brunt of my stress as I managed a marketing agency full-time and did two books "on the side." Thanks to my mother, Barbara LeBlanc, who cheered me on when I felt I couldn't do all this anymore. And thanks to my daughter, Rachel Anderson, for always being in my corner. I work to inspire the change I want to see for you and your sisters in the world.

And of course every woman needs her friends and confidantes. Thank you, Karen Hagewood and Kathryn Bowsher, for always being there for me.

This book would not be possible without several members of my production team. Thanks to Gabriela Martinez, who designed the book cover. To Laura Boyle, who designed the book interior. To Kay Paumier, who kept the content clean and clear. And to Olivia Dippon, who helped keep the project moving and on track. Without you, this book would not have happened.

Most of all, I want to thank all the female founders and their allies for soldiering on, despite the odds. You make a difference. This book is for you.

Let us change the tides together.

Onwards,

Jenn LeBlanc

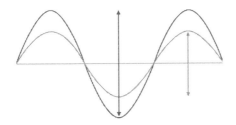

Contents

Introduction

By Jennifer S. LeBlanc

ThinkResults Marketing

THE STATISTICS ARE COMPELLING. Female founders receive little support from venture capitalists (only 2.2 percent of funding in 2017 according to PitchBook). And, when female founders do get funding for their companies, they receive much smaller checks. The average deal for a female founder is a little over $5 million. For a man, it's a little under $12 million.

Why are these statistics so low? One major reason is that there are so few female venture capitalists. In 2017, women represented only eight percent of investors in the top 100 VC firms.

The data for female founders and female funders are inextricably linked, as having more women in both positions would provide more opportunities to change a way of thinking with deeply embedded unconscious bias. Today's culture excludes the thinking and experiences of half the population. As a biologist, I cannot believe that all the best ideas, all the grit, and all the best products and services will come from white guys who have dropped out of Ivy League schools. The odds of that being true are ridiculous. Yet this is the model many VCs use for making funding decisions.

Why does this matter? The most basic answer is that the decisions VCs make affect the technologies we and our kids will use. And, as we all know, those technologies can impact almost every aspect of our lives. So what happens in those closed-door funding sessions matters to each and every one of us. If we want products and services that meet our needs, support our priorities and make a difference in the world, those products and services have to get off the drawing board and into the real world. And that takes money.

THE BUSINESS CASE FOR GENDER DIVERSITY

What makes the funding disparity so compelling (and puzzling) is that female-led companies are, by and large, more successful than male-dominated ones. A growing body of evidence suggests that companies run by female founders are more likely to be profitable investments.

For example, in June 2018, Boston Consulting Group released a report about the gender investment gap. The numbers are astonishing:

> *"According to our research, when women business owners pitch their ideas to investors for early-stage capital, they receive significantly less—a disparity that averages more than $1 million—than men. Yet businesses founded by women ultimately deliver higher revenue—more than twice as much per dollar invested—than those founded by men, making women-owned companies better investments for financial backers."*

This research was conducted in partnership with MassChallenge, a U.S.-based global network of accelerators. MassChallenge has backed more than 1,500 businesses, which have raised more than $3 billion in funding and created more than 80,000 jobs. The report shared several other interesting findings:

1. **Women receive less funding.**
   "Investments in companies founded or cofounded by women averaged $935,000, which is less than half the average $2.1 million invested in companies founded by male entrepreneurs."

2. **Female-founded companies perform better.**
   "Despite this disparity, startups founded and cofounded by women
   actually performed better over time, generating 10 percent more in cumulative revenue over a five-year period: $730,000 compared with
   $662,000."

3. **Investing in female-founded companies leads to higher revenues.**
   "In terms of how effectively companies turn a dollar of investment into
   a dollar of revenue, startups founded and cofounded by women are
   significantly better financial investments. For every dollar of funding,
   these startups generated 78 cents, while male-founded startups generated less than half that - just 31 cents."

Boston Consulting Group is not the only organization finding results like this. Kevin O'Leary, an investor from the TV series "Shark
Tank," has invested in more than 40 companies across the show's nine
seasons. Fully 95 percent of the female-founded companies he invested in reached their financial targets, while only 65 percent of their
male-founded counterparts did so.

A 2018 report from McKinsey reported that companies that are in
the top quartile for gender diversity are 15 percent more likely to have
financial returns above their respective national industry medians. It
follows that having a more diverse set of viewpoints makes it more
likely that an organization will be more flexible, more responsive, and
more likely to reflect the needs and values of its customers. All that
leads to stronger performance.

The research continues to pile up, yet it seems that the data are consistently swept under the rug. It's hard to understand why, in an industry plagued with poor returns (VC funds typically perform worse than
the S&P), the money is not following the money. Female-led companies perform better and return more money to their investors. So why
don't women get more funding?

HOW FEMALE FOUNDERS ARE QUESTIONED VERSUS MEN

One possible reason is the type of questions women are asked. (Yes, you read that right.)

Recently a group of social science researchers analyzed the Question and Answer period following a well-known pitch competition, TechCrunch Disrupt New York City, from 2010 through 2016 to understand the female founder experience better. According to their study, published in the *Harvard Business Review*, 66 percent of the time female founders were asked what the researchers called "prevention-oriented" questions, which focused on "safety, responsibility, security and vigilance." Male founders, on the other hand, were asked "promotion-oriented" questions 67 percent of the time. These questions focused on "hopes, achievement, advancement and ideals."

The authors reported, "The financiers rhetorically produce stereotypical images of women as having qualities opposite to those considered important to being an entrepreneur, with VCs questioning their credibility, trustworthiness, experience, and knowledge."

TOPIC	PROMOTION	PREVENTION
Customers	Acquisition: "How do you want to acquire customers?"	Retention: "How many daily and monthly active users do you have?"
Income Statement	Sales: "How do you plan to monetize this?	Margins: "How long will it take to break even?"
Market	Size: "Do you think that your target market is growing?"	Share: "Is it a defensible business wherein other people can't come into the space to take share?"
Projections	Growth: "What major milestones are you targeting this year?"	Stability: "How predictable are your future cash flows?"
Strategy	Vision: "What's the brand vision?"	Execution: "Are you planning to Turing test this?"
Management	Entrepreneur: "Can you tell us a bit about yourself?"	Team: "How much of this are you actually doing in-house?"

Courtesy of *Harvard Business Review*; See Kanze, Huang, Conley & Higgins, 2017, 2018.

After this pitch contest, women received 25 percent of the funding they had requested, while men received more than half of the funding they had requested.

I thought two other findings in this study were particularly interesting. The first was sobering. For every prevention-oriented question, founders raised $3.8 million LESS in funding. This is after the researchers corrected for every other possible variable, including the age of the company, the experience of the founder, and the like. The only difference was the type of question asked. Since women received more prevention-type questions, it follows that they raised less money than their male counterparts.

The second interesting finding was that there are ways around prevention-oriented questions.

Some background. It is human nature to answer a question in a similar manner to the way the question is asked. This means that founders tend to give promotion-oriented answers to promotion-oriented questions, and to give prevention-oriented answers to prevention-oriented questions.

However, some founders did not respond to the prevention questions in kind. They turned the answers around to make them promotion-oriented. Those founders who gave mostly promotion-oriented answers to prevention-oriented questions raised an average of **$7.9 million in total funding**. This is compared to those who responded more typically to prevention-oriented questions with prevention-oriented answers. They raised an average of just $563,000. That translates to a more than 14x increase in funding simply by turning the questions around. That's an astounding finding and an empowering piece of data.

Here's an example of how this might work in practice. Let's say an investor asks you, "So how are you going to protect your market share in a crowded space?" The founder can answer, "That's a good question and it's important to be concerned with market share. However, our focus is primarily on growing our market share. Let me tell you about the three ways we plan to do that." And then the founder can talk about plans and aspiration (performance-oriented topics). A prevention-oriented question, respectfully converted into a promotion-oriented answer, will gain you, on average, 14x more funding. Knowledge is power.

FEMALE FOUNDERS ARE SUCCEEDING DESPITE THE ODDS

That skill in turning around negative questions may be part of the reason that, despite the odds stacked against them, many female founders are succeeding, and even running multi-million- and multi-billion-dollar startups. For example, Adi Tatarko leads Houzz, a home-remodeling marketplace company valued at $4 billion. TaskRabbit, a marketplace for personal-support services led by Stacy Philpot-Brown, was valued at $38 million just before its sale to IKEA. Katrina Lake leads StitchFix, a subscription clothing business valued at $2 billion. Jennifer Hyman runs Rent the Runway, a clothing rental company valued at $800 million.

Also, there is a lot of chatter in the Valley about several up-and-coming female-founded firms expected to break the unicorn* barrier in the next few years. The tide is changing.

THINGS ARE GETTING BETTER

Fortunately, there have been some important positive changes. There are now numerous initiatives across the VC and founder communities to ensure that there is better representation in the female VC community and that female founders will receive better support and mentorship.

For example, Emily Chang released her book *Brotopia: Breaking Up the Boys' Club of Silicon Valley* in February 2018. That book examined the area's toxic masculinity and its impact on all of us.

In March 2018, Alpha Edison issued a challenge to VCs in honor of International Women's Day: Meet with eight women in March whom you haven't met with before. The idea is that funding is a relationship business and you will not fund someone you don't know. So widen your circle. Many VCs firms pledged to do that in March. I hope that they continue that every month. It's not a lot but every change begins with a crack in the rock.

---

* The term "unicorn", coined by Aileen Lee of Cowboy Ventures, describes a small company that dramatically increases its market capitalization to $1 billion or so.

In 2017, 34 senior female VCs founded All Raise with the goal to turn around the numbers for female founders and funders. One of their key initiatives is gathering the data around these issues, which is the first step to understanding the problem. All Raise (www.AllRaise.org) formalized cells of activity including Female Founders Office Hours, a program to introduce more female founders to VCs across the U.S.; and #FoundersforChange, a group of founders who refuse to take money from VCs who refuse to be inclusive. All Raise was started by Aileen Lee. Maha Ibrahim, a contributor to *Changing Tides,* is a member. (Note: A portion of the proceeds of *Changing Tides* will be donated to All Raise.)

And increasingly we have places where we find like-minded investors who openly and expressly support female founders so that we can bring more ideas, products, services and companies conceived and built by women into the world, such as:

- Google Launchpad Female Founders Summit
- Female Founders Community on Facebook
- Women's Startup Lab
- *Fortune*'s list of the top 100 VC firms with females and percentages, including the growth in new firms led by women and in the corporate venture arena
- Watermark (San Francisco Bay Area)
- Lean In Circles
- UPWARD chapters across the U.S.
- And more.

WHERE DO WE GO FROM HERE?

So there is hope. What happens next?

The first step to making a change is to understand the problem. The second step is to examine ways the problem can be solved, or at least mediated.

That's where this book comes in. I knew this book had to happen, and I asked every female VC, every female founder, and every ecosystem partner I knew to be a part of it. This book represents a spectrum of important voices as we change the tides. I wanted to bring together these points of light that were happening in isolation and throw a big spotlight on these voices.

Here you'll find a description of the problem, with lots of personal stories, statistics and other compelling information.

You'll also find suggestions on how to tackle this problem—practical and tactical tips that female founders can use to ensure smooth (or at least smoother) sailing when looking for funding for the next generation of companies.

We hope this book will be valuable for many of you, including:

- Female founders and would-be founders, to help you understand you are not alone, and to give you tools and techniques to help you succeed. My hope is that this book will be your lifeline, that you will grab it when you feel like giving up, and that you will find the inspiration you need within its pages.
- Any investor, to help you select and nurture the companies that will make a difference and make a profit.
- Women struggling to fit into male-dominated businesses, which are definitely not restricted to Silicon Valley.
- The guys who "get it" and who "want to get it," who support women in business and in life.

Specifically, here's what you'll find in this book:

- Maha Ibrahim (Canaan Partners) shares her experience and insights as an immigrant woman investor.
- Gillian Muessig (Sybilla Masters Fund) advises us how to find unicorns in uncrowded fields.
- Terri (Hanson) Mead (Class Bravo Ventures) advocates creating a mesh network to connect female founders and like-minded investors to invest in female founders.
- Xandra Laskowski (OSEA Angel Investors) gives advice on how to be a successful angel investor.
- Suzanne Fletcher (Stanford StartX Fund) explains how joining a community can dramatically improve your chances of success.

- Amy Belt Raimundo (Kaiser Permanente Ventures) advises how to turn the fact that you will often be the only woman in the room into your advantage.
- Mukund Mohan (BuildDirect Technologies) points out that women have a distinct advantage—higher user (customer) empathy—that can translate into better startup outcomes.
- Deb Kilpatrick (Evidation Health) gives tips on how to be tenacious and gracious when raising capital.
- Dorin Rosenshine (Outleads) discusses the joys and pitfalls of being a solo female founder.
- Tammy Bowers (Lionheart Innovations) examines 10 rules for living life both as a founder and a mother.
- Robyn Ward (Founder*Forward*) examines the relationship of self-care to success, and gives tips on how to get your life back on track, especially after you get funded.
- Jessica Livingston (Y Combinator) examines what it takes to be a massively successful unicorn.
- Kate Purmal (Georgetown University Women's Leadership Institute) examines the importance of vision in transitioning from entrepreneur to executive leader.
- Debra Vernon (VLP Law Group) further develops the business case for investing in women-lead startups.

My goal and the goal of the other contributors in the book is to raise awareness of the problem and to examine possible solutions. Yes, we want to help right the wrongs. However, we want to do more than that. We want to change the tide to build a more inclusive and profitable future for all of us.

SOURCES

BCG
Abouzahr, Katie, Frances Brooks Taplett, Matt Krentz, and John Harthorne. "Why Women-Owned Startups Are a Better Bet." June 6, 2018. https://www.bcg.com/en-us/ publications/2018/why-women-owned-startups-are-better-bet.aspx.

First Round
"First Round 10 Year Project." *First Round 10 Year Project*, www.10years.firstround.com/.

Fortune
Zarya, Valentina. "Female Founders Got 2% of Venture Capital Dollars in 2017." **Fortune**, January 31, 2018. www.fortune.com/2018/01/31/female-founders-venture-capital-2017.

HBR
Conley, Mark A., Dana Kanze, Laura Huang and E. Tory Higgins. "Male and Female Entrepreneurs Get Asked Different Questions by VCs - and It Affects How Much Funding They Get." *Harvard Business Review*, September 20, 2017. www. hbr.org/2017/06/male-and-female-entrepreneurs-get-asked-different-questions-by-vcs-and-it-affects-how-much-funding-they-get.

Kevin O'Leary
Canal, Emily. "'Kevin O'Leary: Why I Prefer to Invest in Women-Led Businesses." *Inc.com*, September 26, 2017. www.inc.com/emily-canal/kevin-oleary-women-led-companies-shark-tank-inc-womens-summit.html.

McKinsey
Hunt, Vivian, Dennis Layton, and Sara Prince. "Why Diversity Matters." *McKinsey & Company*, February 2015, www.mckinsey.com/business-functions/organization/our-insights/why-diversity-matters.

TechCrunch

Teare, Gené, and Ned Desmond. "Announcing the 2017 Update to the Crunchbase Women in Venture Report." *TechCrunch*, October 4, 2017, www.techcrunch.com/2017/10/04/announcing-the-2017-update-to-the-crunchbase-women-in-venture-report/.

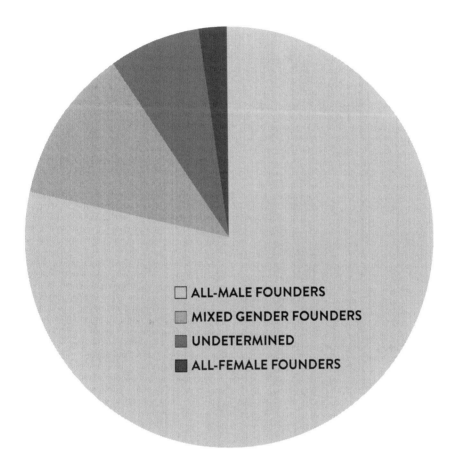

☐ ALL-MALE FOUNDERS

▨ MIXED GENDER FOUNDERS

▨ UNDETERMINED

▨ ALL-FEMALE FOUNDERS

All female-founded teams received 2.2% of VC funding, compared to 79% for all-male teams, 12% for mixed-gender teams and 7% for teams whose gender PitchBook was unable to confirm (2017)

Source: *Fortune* and PitchBook

fortune.com/2018/01/31/female-founders-venture-capital-2017

Changing Tides:
Investing to Change the Tide

By Maha Ibrahim
Canaan Partners

THINGS HAVE CHANGED a lot since I started my career as an investor in Silicon Valley. When I came to Canaan Partners 17 years ago, I was the first and only woman on the Canaan investment team. Now the team is 40 percent female and three of the eight general partners are women. This is highly unusual in the venture capital world. This also means that each person on the Canaan team has invested in a female-founded company, another extremely rare and unusual situation. At this time, 25 percent of our portfolio companies are founded by women. This compares to the current industry average of 11 percent of investments in female-led startups.

At Canaan Partners, we focus on early-stage, series A investments. Our current fund – Canaan 11 – is an $800 million fund which will be invested over a three-year period. The investment strategy we apply is to go early and get high ownership, ensuring that Canaan is the first large institutional capital to be invested.

Our team has a disciplined investment strategy and our portfolio reflects an investment ratio of 40 percent healthcare and 60 percent technology. We go deeply over a long period of time to embed ourselves in the sector and the community, so that we are able to see when something new comes up and act quickly.

Our newest investment sector is Frontier Tech (aerospace), which offers us the opportunities to invest in the "next big thing." One of our successful early investments was Skybox, a satellite-imaging firm in which Canaan invested $18 million. It was acquired by Google in 2014 for $500 million.

I have worked on a handful of other projects in the areas of cutting-edge robotics, driverless vehicles, and computing. The powerful benefit of the aerospace sector is that truly transformational tech and ideas are being developed. It's also less competitive for VCs than consumer or enterprise-facing sectors. We look for the open space and take advantage of opportunities there.

"WOMEN ARE LESS AMBITIOUS"

Over the years, I've seen some fairly extreme biases toward female founders, and these are often difficult to break when it comes to non-consumer, non-healthcare industries such as enterprise software, infrastructure, frontier tech, and other "non-traditional" industries. Women are frequently asked questions like "Why are you the CEO?" and "How do you know this business?" They are questioned in ways a man would never be questioned. As we see more women entrepreneurs in these areas, I hope that those biases will go away. More women need to get into these fields and represent themselves, and we need to support the women who are already in these industries, and make sure they succeed.

I have also heard male investors say things like "women are less ambitious" and that women "tend to shoot for the moon instead of the stars." These are incredibly unfortunate thoughts that we will overcome as we see more female success stories.

For me, the exposure of the extreme sexism in the VC world began with Ellen Pao's sexual harassment trial against Kleiner Perkin Caufield and Byers. She had such incredible strength to speak her truth against the most storied of Silicon Valley VC firms. To do what had kept every woman quiet before her—risk her career and her reputation. So brave and groundbreaking. I followed the trial with intense interest as did many women in Silicon Valley. Then came Susan Fowler and her honest portrayal of life at Uber, which led to the ousting of the then CEO Travis Kalanick.

But it wasn't until the sexual harassment claims against Justin Caldbeck, general partner at Binary Capital led to the unravelling of that company, that Silicon Valley began to take this whole issue seriously. Before this, many articles were written and "rumors spread" because they were titillating and got clicks for their publishers. People simply considered these incidents to be isolated and not a big concern.

Following the Justin Caldbeck situation in summer 2017, and then Dave McClure of 500 Startups, so many other men in tech began to be exposed for their sexual harassment behavior and, in some cases, flat-out sexual abuse and assault. These revelations, combined with a waterfall of so many voices coming out one by one during the #metoo movement starting in the fall of 2017, really changed the conversation in Silicon Valley. I have such respect for all of the women who were strong enough to make their voices heard. They made a difference.

In addition to the women who spoke out, social media played a positive and powerful role in rallying people quickly around this issue, spreading the news and connecting people together in a shared experience. The #metoo movement, which started somewhat after the meltdown in the VC and tech community over sexual harassment, wouldn't have been so quick and so widespread without the benefit of social networks. They have been incredibly helpful at bringing this issue to light and amplifying the message for those who had the courage to speak. For this I am grateful.

BEING A WOMAN IS A DISTINCT ADVANTAGE

One advantage I have as a woman, especially at this time, is that it gives me an edge with female founders. I have women coming through my door daily who have had bad experiences with other VCs and investors. I hear their stories of biases, of discrimination, of being ignored and dismissed solely because they are women. I have funded at least four founders who have stories of walking into other firms and being treated as less than their male counterparts. I am given opportunities to see the potential for companies and founders that other investors have dismissed or overlooked, allowing me to build strong and valuable relationships with the founders.

Multiple studies have shown that when a woman is at the investment table, investment firms are much more likely to invest in female-founded companies. They are, in fact, two to three times more likely to receive funding if there is at least one woman on the investment team. We offer female founders that opportunity. I believe that female founders will feel more welcome and will bring in more good ideas if they have female investors with whom they can connect.

Despite the issues that women have experienced here in Silicon Valley, I have never felt that being the only woman in the room is a disadvantage. I have learned to use my voice in a way that is opinionated and reasoned, to have conversations that aren't about emotions, but rather about doing the right thing. I have also learned to throw down the hammer when it is important. My nickname has often been "the velvet hammer." I am living proof that investment firms can change, evolve for the better and still perform – or even outperform the competition. I hope that the recent trend of hiring more female investment professionals is actually going to change things, and it's not just a fad.

When everyone comes at something from the same side you have a limited lens. Women often don't have access to funds because the investment table isn't open to them. I look for diversity at the investment table – a larger, more diverse lens will lead to greater success.

BEING AN IMMIGRANT IS ALSO A COMPETITIVE ADVANTAGE

One other thing that defines me is that I am a first-generation immigrant. My parents immigrated to the United States from Egypt. I feel that it gives me an advantage, an extra bit of drive and hunger to achieve more. I have found that oftentimes immigrants have something to prove; that's what I'm looking for as an investor, and an employer. I look for people who are intelligent, driven, nimble, and who will hustle.

I have been responsible for hiring many of the analysts at Canaan and most of them are immigrants or first-generation professionals. This wasn't an intentional choice, I saw the same drive and motivation in them that has driven my success. Sociology tells us that we like homogenous groups, a preference that manifests itself in surrounding yourself with people who have similar experiences. For me that homogeneity is immigrant and first-generation Americans who have the same drive and motivation that I do to achieve something greater.

I have invested in several immigrant-founded companies, which is unusual both in the VC realm and at Canaan. I want people who have the drive and don't have a safety net to fall back on, who will give everything to be successful. Startups are hard, and I need people who are going to get beyond the walls and reach the goal, who will do whatever is needed to achieve their goal. I often see that drive and intensity in immigrant founders.

WHAT I'M LOOKING FOR IN INVESTMENTS

I invest in early-stage opportunities so a key thing I am looking for is "How big is the market?" and "How quickly and how well can you attack that market?" The size and timing of the market are critical. It doesn't matter if you have the greatest product or idea if the market is not ready for it.

As an investor, it is about the ambition and the opportunity set that you offer. Market size is first, followed by timing, then by your differentiator in that market. When you are pitching, you need to make the VCs believe that they will be successful and make money by investing in your business. You want the VCs to become what I call a "Belieber" (aka a Justin Bieber fan) – they need to become your zealot by the time your pitch is done.

The thing I struggle with most in the Silicon Valley ecosystem is the hype. I recognize the value of it from a business perspective, but I crave substance and authenticity that is severely lacking in the Valley. So, yes,

I am also looking for founders who are authentic, who truly believe in what they are trying to create.

WHAT IS SUCCESS?

This is an important question we all need to ask ourselves and find our own answer: "When are you a success?" I have reached the point where I'm able to wake up each morning and say to myself "Everything is all good." The drive is still there, but it's not as demanding as it used to be. I have learned to accept myself and reflect on my accomplishments.

Over the years I've experienced periods of insecurity. When I had my sons, now 10 and 11, it was difficult for me to take the time off. Of course, no one told me that I could take as much time as I needed, and I constantly felt the stress and insecurity of my situation. For three years, I felt that I was doing everything at only 70 percent — I was a 70 percent mom, a 70 percent partner at Canaan. I wasn't able to give myself the freedom to acknowledge that I was doing the best that I could at the time.

Looking back, I know that it was because I had my eye on the prize, that I wasn't settled, that I knew that I could excel even more. Now I realize that the goals I had set were unattainable, and I have come to terms with that.

As bystanders supporting female founders, it can be incredibly hard to look beyond certain circumstances, especially when you are also caught up in the situation. It's important to not talk to female founders about maternity, motherhood, or how to figure out how they can "do it all." It's more helpful to talk about looking beyond work and what each woman needs to do to take care of herself.

I have learned to look beyond the current situation and to give myself the freedom and space to succeed and fail. This is especially true for my professional life: the VC business is more about failure than it is about success. If you are going to be in this business, you have to become comfortable with failure. I have learned to be more okay with that than I used to be.

MENTORING THE NEXT GENERATION OF FOUNDERS AND INVESTORS

Mentorship is an important topic for me, especially for women in Silicon Valley. I didn't have a mentor or sponsor when I started my career here – for me, it was trial by fire. I would never wish that experience on anyone, but it has taught me how to treat others. It has reinforced to me that it's all about empathy.

Over the years, I have been involved in many types of mentorship, from supporting students to working with the State Department on international women entrepreneurs coming to the U.S. I've also been involved for many years with Sonja Perkins' Broadway Angels, a female angel network made up mostly of general partners who invest in female-led companies.

Right now, I'm involved with a group of female general partners who are trying to see what we can do to remedy the lack of diversity in our industry. While we began working back in 2017, we launched the AllRaise.org website in April of 2018. We are dedicated to diversity in funders and founders. We are focused on supporting and informing women founders about how and when to raise capital, if it's the right choice for them, what the next steps are, and answering many other questions to encourage more women to seek and find funding.

> "If there is one thing we can learn from Ellen Pao, Susan Fowler and every woman who shared her #metoo story to shed light on this issue, it is to make sure your voice is heard."

Lots of women are being hired at this time in reaction to the latest news and the ripples throughout firms in the Valley, but to me it's not enough that they are being hired at the junior level. Together with Time's Up, we will be organizing events for investment professionals who are interested in moving from analyst positions to more senior positions, such as general partner. We will focus on mentoring, career progression, negotiating styles, family, balance, and help to answer questions like "What's the follow-up?" and "What comes next?"

We need to make sure that the junior members who want to stay in the industry are able to do so. By mid-career, most women have left because they were being treated badly and were tired of it, and either got out of investing completely or started their own firms. I see it as my responsibility to help keep the women entering our industry to stay in the industry. The worst thing would be to have more women come in and then have them leave – why would they stay here if they're being treated badly?

CREATING THE VC 2.0 COMMUNITY

The changes I have seen in Silicon Valley in the last year have been monumental, and we still have lots of work to do. If there is one thing we can learn from Ellen Pao, Susan Fowler and every woman who shared her #metoo story to shed light on this issue, it is to make sure your voice is heard. Be present and have an opinion. You might be wrong, and that's fine. Learn the most authentic way that you can persuade and do it. Your special persuasive power might be pounding your fist on the table, sharing your views via a presentation, writing a blog about your experiences, whatever works for you. Find your strength and speak out. You cannot be mute. Be prepared and don't be quiet.

As an investor, I work to do the same, to develop a strong voice in this community, and a strong influence. I am heartened by the changes I have seen in Silicon Valley during my time here, and particularly over the last few years. This includes how these issues are being shown in social media and in the media at large. Women are being heard and are becoming a force to be reckoned with in business and as founders. I am excited that people are starting to understand that a lack of females in the workforce has a limiting effect on the work we do here in Silicon Valley in bringing new technologies and solutions to the market.

The next step is to figure out how we can promote and retain people of diverse backgrounds, both as investors and as founders. That is the open question I have (and one that needs to be answered soon). I am optimistic. I have said that when I lose my optimism I should retire – optimism and realism are the keys to being a good investor. And so, I remain optimistic.

Maha Ibrahim spots technology trends early and partners closely with her companies to drive growth and exits. She focuses on e-commerce and enterprise / cloud, and was one of the first investors to recognize the potential of social gaming. A champion of women in technology, Maha is passionate about funding and raising the profiles of female entrepreneurs and is a founding member of All Raise. She is also a trustee for the Carnegie Endowment for International Peace. Maha holds a B.A. in economics and an M.A. in sociology from Stanford University, and a Ph.D. in economics from MIT.

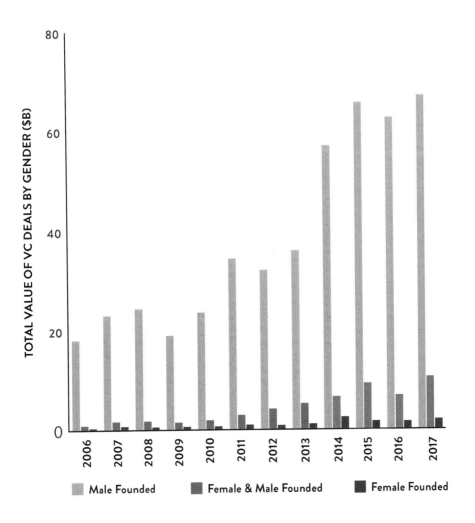

Except for 2014, 2017 marks the largest percentage of total venture dollars directed toward female founders (2.2%) since 2006, when PitchBook began tracking this data.

Source: Fortune and PitchBook
http://fortune.com/2018/01/31/female-founders-venture-capital-2017/

Seeking Unicorns in Uncrowded Fields

By Gillian Muessig

Sybilla Masters Fund | Outlines Venture Group

2.19 PERCENT: a number that has a lot of blood boiling. That's the percentage of traditional venture funding that was invested in female founders in 2017. A little more went to diverse-gender founding teams. Almost all traditional venture funding is awarded to tall, Caucasian, young males from either Stanford or Harvard, speaking fluent American English, with baritone voices. Everything and everyone else are "points off" in this game.

WOMEN ARE OUTPERFORMING, DESPITE THE ODDS

Women are at a disadvantage at every point in the journey. During due diligence meetings, VCs ask men "forward-looking" questions such as, "What are your plans for capturing the market?" Women are asked prevention and disaster-containment questions, such as "How will you prevent customer churn?"

Women are funded less frequently, at lower valuations, and receive less capital per investment. They must launch, prove their markets, and expand with less capital. They have fewer role models, mentors, and champions. They are at a constant disadvantage compared to their male colleagues.

And yet, report after report indicates that women outperform their male counterparts and return higher ROI to their investors. First Round Capital's now famous 2015 report notes that, over the previous decade, women-led companies returned 63 percent higher ROI to their investors.

Kevin O'Leary reviewed Shark Tank's investments and noted that "95 percent of the women-led companies met their financial targets, compared with just 65 percent for businesses with male leaders." Men were setting targets that were not achievable. "Women don't waste time," he asserted. Even more damning, O'Leary continues, "I don't have a single company run by a man right now that's outperformed the ones run by women."

In the publicly held company arena, *Fortune Magazine* reported that "women CEOs in the *Fortune* 1000 drive three times the returns as S&P 500 enterprises run predominantly by men."

One would think the money would be following the money. As of 2018, it still is not.

UNCONSCIOUS BIAS IS MORE POWERFUL THAN YOU THOUGHT

In his book, *Strangers to Ourselves,* Timothy Wilson writes that the subconscious human brain processes about 11 million bits of information per second. By comparison, the conscious brain processes about 40 bits of information. It's no wonder that unconscious bias affects every situation, discussion, and decision we make throughout our lives.

And well it should. Studies by the Ontario Institute for Studies in Education (OISE) at the University of Toronto show that six- to nine-month-old infants are already more inclined to learn information from someone of the same race than from an adult of a different race. This unconscious bias to pay attention to, bond to, and learn from people who are most like ourselves has strong roots. It helped human infants stick close to their parents, rather than wander off with other mammals. Human babies don't survive long if they start cozying up to lions, hyenas, and bears.

That same vestigial survival mechanism backfires in a world thousands of years later, in which diverse teams consistently bring in higher ROI. This conversation is not just about gender diversity. Janice Machala, a longtime startup investor in Puget Sound, says she only invests in diverse founding teams because diversity at the leadership level is a proxy for a leadership team that can listen to and act on diverse ideas. Diverse leaders make companies more resilient and more capable of acquiring new markets more efficiently.

Diverse founding teams that consistently demonstrate their ability to survive tough times and expand with capital efficiency give investors a powerful incentive to invest.

GENDER-LENS INVESTING

Gender-lens investing is the deliberate integration of gender analysis into investment analysis and decision making. Jackie VanderBrug, managing director at Bank of America Global Wealth Management, provides a good synopsis of the subject.

> Gender-lens investing illuminates on the lenses through which we observe the value of companies, not on limitations or exclusions.
>
> For example, how can a company benefit from debiasing their software design, which has traditionally been designed for male patterns of problem solving, to include people of all genders with diverse sets of problem-solving skills?
>
> When we are aware of the biases we bring to our review process, we are able to make better investment decisions.

INVESTING IN UNCROWDED FIELDS

As an investor, I look at the fact that more than 97 percent of funding is controlled by – and awarded to – all-male, largely Caucasian teams who graduated from Stanford or Harvard. Not only does that speak of uncontrolled unconscious bias, it leads to over-inflated valuations and over-invested sectors.

"A" grade deals are being overlooked in under-served locations, built by overlooked founding teams, and in market sectors beyond the few that get all the current attention of Silicon Valley, New York, and London. It stands to reason that there is money to be made by seeking out unicorns in uncrowded fields.

VENTURE CAPITAL IS NOT BROKEN

Venture capital was designed to – and does a good job of – funding the ideas that power the "next big thing." That's why this year's buzzwords are artificial intelligence (AI), Internet of Things (IoT), augmented reality (AR), virtual reality (VR) and blockchain. As an investor, I observe that the "A" deals are forged behind closed doors by a small group of men who have known each other for 20 or more years. The rest of us lowly individual investors don't get to play. At best, we can invest at the angel stage, before the VCs have seen the deal. If we are lucky enough to find, and wise enough to invest in a unicorn or near-unicorn company before the VCs get on board, our returns will still be whittled away with each successive venture round.

> " ... report after report is rolling in indicating that women are outperforming their male counterparts and returning higher ROI to their investors."

Many angel investment groups hang around the edges of the cool kids' club of powerful VCs. Snug and full of tasty luncheons, angel group members review home-grown "B" and "C" quality deals, thinking they are "A" deals, because they don't know the difference.

AVERAGE ROI FOR ANGELS: 0 TO 12%

Carlee Price of Pique Financial Works did a deep dive into the actual returns angel investors are seeing from their efforts. She recently reported that the average angel investment returns hover between 0 and 12 percent, with many angel investors seeing negative returns. Angel groups routinely report returns of 22 to 30 percent, attracting new investors to join their ranks. Where's the disconnect?

Dean Rosenberg, president of Tech Coast Angels (TCA) San Diego, explained it clearly to me. He said that a few investors put early money into a couple of companies that later had near-billion-dollar exits. Those few investors made a lot of money. The balance of the companies TCA San Diego looked at over the years didn't amount to much. Some had modest exits; others failed. The few investors who made a killing on the big deals skewed the entire group's average.

Here the difference between *mean* and *average* is extremely important. Even if the *mean* return for an angel investor were 12 percent, the ROI is completely insufficient for the risk of the asset class. In my hometown of Seattle, I hear grumbling from private investors who have money in some of the most respected VCs in town. They are not thrilled with the returns they are getting.

The average time for an IPO exit is 11 to 15 years, not two to three, or even three to five years as it was a few decades ago. The average individual investor is in their midlife or a bit older. Unless your money is inherited, it generally takes time to accumulate the wealth that makes you a qualified investor. That means you get to play the early-stage venture investment game about twice in your lifetime. And the second time around, if you're my age, you'll be so old, you won't care.

From the entrepreneur's side, traditional venture capital is not all it's cracked up to be either. In his book, *Lost and Founder,* Rand Fishkin, cofounder of Moz, notes that once you accept even a single dollar of venture capital, you agree to sell or grow your company to an IPO as quickly as possible. He writes: "The only way the 5 percent of successful VCs make their returns is through enormous outcomes from a tiny number of companies. Get comfortable with the odds or don't roll the dice."

Scores of pundits complain that venture capital is broken. I suggest that it is not. It simply isn't the only startup investment vehicle we need.

In the 1990s the web showed up conveniently at the end of a millennium. We had millennial conversations: "We have a universe, unfettered by the laws of math and time! How shall we populate it?" We had a lot of fun batting around in that new brave new World Wide Web. But now, the pilings are in place. From a business standpoint, the web looks a lot more like a playing field than an empty universe. Now our questions should be, "How shall we leverage the web to build better ways to live and work together?"

While there are an increasing number of unicorn companies over time, very few startups are designed to be venture fundable. Still, entrepreneurs are solving some of the world's most pressing problems and many will make solid, reliable companies that enhance their communities and support the people who engage with them as employees, vendors, and consumers.

This phenomenon engenders the need for us to design better ways to get our early-stage venture investment money in and out for both the investor and the entrepreneur.

BETTER WAYS TO LIVE AND WORK TOGETHER

Lighter Capital is doing well by offering factoring loans with a twist. If your company has minimum gross revenues of at least $15,000 a month, you can obtain an expansion capital loan and make payments from a percentage of top-line revenues until the loan is paid in full. These loans are essentially factoring, painted with a fancy new name and brought into the 21st century. They carry high interest rates, making them profitable to the lender. Since monthly payments are determined by top-line revenues received each month, the payments remain reasonably affordable to the borrower company throughout the life of the loan. Taking this kind of funding can keep the CAP table clean and does not hog-tie senior management into working toward a certain exit or IPO.

At Outlines Venture Group, we look for mutually beneficial ways to fund companies. To that end, we launched the Sybilla Masters Fund, a gender-lens investment fund, with the goal of raising a $100 million fund chartered to source, fund, and support companies with at least one dominant female founder – a woman in a position of strategic and operational control. Balancing gender representation in senior management sounds like a social goal. Based on growing evidence, it is also a financially sound decision. In this focus, we join about a dozen such groups around the country and a growing number around the world, ranging from Aspect Ventures, Backstage Capital and Broadway Angels to Astia, Golden Seeds, and others.

Venture capital investing needs a scalpel these days, not a hatchet. To meet the needs of a wider variety of companies around the world, we offer a myriad of funding options, bringing nuance to venture funding, thereby serving the needs of many more entrepreneurs. We offer debt instruments, such as revenue-share loans and dividend-based options. We invest using traditional equity methods, and we have debt + equity hybrid options as well.

EVERYONE ON DECK; THERE ARE PROBLEMS TO BE SOLVED

At the 2017 G20 Leaders' Summit, Angel Gurría, secretary general of the Organization for Economic Cooperation and Development (OECD) said, "Women are the most underutilized economic asset in the world's economy." The entire world stands to gain trillions of dollars in annual economic value by giving women equal opportunity to engage in entrepreneurial efforts and leadership roles.

Melinda Gates, co-founder of the Bill and Melinda Gates Foundation, investor, and philanthropist, agrees, "I am convinced that we'll never reach our goals if we don't also address the systematic way that women and girls are undervalued."

Anne Nguyen, partner and managing director at The Boston Consulting Group, drives home the message: "Diversity isn't just a social or political movement. It is a business imperative, both in terms of the potential implications, but also the potential to drive higher innovation and returns through diversity."

Unconscious bias and historically patriarchal systems are ineffective models for making investment decisions. The time has come to bring not only our unconscious biases to our decision-making processes, but also methodologies for recognizing that bias and to consciously review companies, teams, problems, solutions, and opportunities through new lenses that will lead to better companies and communities, as well as higher returns for investors.

 *Gillian Muessig is the co-founder of Moz, brettapproved, and Outlines Venture Group, and a general partner at the Sybilla Masters Fund, a gender-lens venture capital fund. Gillian enjoys a global reputation for keeping her finger on the pulse of early-stage startup investment opportunities across established and emerging markets. She serves on boards of directors of technology, biotech and marketing firms on four continents, and has served on the Tech Advisory Board to the Bill and Melinda Gates Foundation. Over the course of her career, Gillian has helped more than 1,000 companies launch, grow, pivot and thrive.*

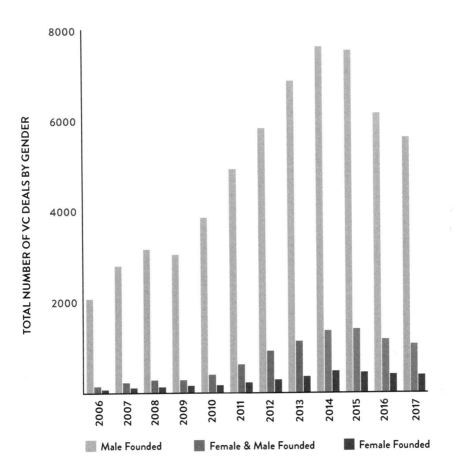

TOTAL NUMBER OF VC DEALS BY GENDER

■ Male Founded   ■ Female & Male Founded   ■ Female Founded

Female-founded companies set a record in 2017, making up 4.4% of all VC deals, the largest percentage since PitchBook started tracking data in 2006.

Source: Fortune and PitchBook

http://fortune.com/2018/01/31/female-founders-venture-capital-2017

Activating the Mesh Network: Female Angels Investing in Female Founders

By Terri (Hanson) Mead

Class Bravo Ventures

I BECAME AN ANGEL INVESTOR in 2015 following a friend's suggestion that I consider it to diversify my business experience. I had been working as a consultant for 10 years, felt pigeon-holed within IT in life sciences, and wanted to learn more about what was going on from a tech perspective in Silicon Valley. I was also looking for a new opportunity to leverage my diverse business experience.

My friend had mentioned Sand Hill Angels, so I decided to go all in without looking at any other angel groups or investing opportunities. I was told by the membership person (who was an old white guy just like my dad) that the Board most likely would not approve my application because I didn't fit the "typical profile." I did not challenge what he meant by "the typical profile." Instead, when my application was approved, I felt I had to prove that I belonged at the table.

LEARNING FROM THE EXPERIENCES OF FEMALE FOUNDERS

It didn't take me long to realize that the female founders who came in to present didn't get the same level of attention as their male counterparts. I watched some of the male investors tune out as soon as the women got to the front of the room. Others tuned out when they saw that the company's product wasn't designed for them. One investor actually asked a female founder why anyone would want the product she was pitching, simply because he couldn't see himself buying it. At this point I realized these investors were typical in their inability to see the potential demand for something they couldn't relate to – and were unwilling to make any effort to understand its market opportunities.

After coaching many female founders on how to pitch to these traditional male investors, I also realized that getting them to shift their strategy would be incredibly difficult despite the emphasis being put on the financial opportunities of the investments. I was hoping to dazzle the investors with dollars, but there was still the hurdle of getting them to see that there was actual demand, or even just getting them to understand the product.

Jennifer Hyman of Rent the Runway often talks about having to spend 30 minutes of a 45-minute meeting explaining the product before she could even get into the business details. And then the investors would respond by saying they would "have to ask their wives" who were not part of Jennifer's demographic and would be terrible points of reference.

HOW DO WE GET MORE MONEY INTO THE HANDS OF FEMALE FOUNDERS?

With over 90 percent of VCs being male and with only 2 percent of VC funding in female founders, it can seem like an insurmountable task to overcome the conscious and unconscious biases that women face on a daily basis. So the question becomes, how do we get more money into the hands of female founders? And where can this funding come from? OK. That's two questions.

The answers lie in us as women. We need more female investors to create a separate funding and support ecosystem. We need female investors to invest in companies, products and services that more closely align with our values. Women tend not to be interested in ROI at all costs and may not know how to invest or how to take more risk. In general, women are more likely to write a philanthropy check than to invest in a startup, and that needs to shift.

Sallie Krawcheck of Ellevest and Ellevate says that, although women live longer than men, we don't take the same level of investing risk and, as such, end up with a major financial gap later in life. Men have the advantage in that they are generally willing to take risks, have better access to the investing opportunities, and are more willing to invest. But they aren't investing in female founders, so we have a double whammy of a problem.

I am excited to see a significant shift on this front. Organizations like Portfolia, Pipeline Angels and Next Wave Ventures are providing low-cost entry into the startup investing ecosystem for women who are accredited investors. I am a bit unusual in that I decided to jump right into the deep end of startup investing (after 20 years of traditional portfolio investing) instead of taking classes, joining Portfolia and easing into it. That's not really my style as I learn by experience and I am a very selective joiner.

Portfolia and Next Wave are similar in that you invest a minimum of $10,000 into a fund and then participate to the extent that you want to in the deal flow, due diligence, negotiations, etc. It's a great way to learn and diversify in that the $10,000 will go into several startups and not just one. My average check size is between $10,000 and $15,000 so that represents one round of investing for me.

I recently heard the number of dollars that will be shifting into the hands of women over the next five to ten years – it was mindboggling. This presents us with a huge opportunity to reallocate funds (or a portion of them) from consumer spending or philanthropy into the startup funding ecosystem for female founders and for products and services that we want to see in this world. This won't happen overnight, so we need to work on getting more women comfortable with taking the risk of investing, more specifically investing in startups.

Unfortunately, the current ecosystem is steeped in the "bro culture," which is hostile toward women. Most of us have experienced sexual harassment and discrimination, whether overt or subtle. That makes it not only difficult—but sometimes impossible—to participate. We are often not in the room when the deals and decisions are made. And, based on recent articles in *Vanity Fair* and *The New York Times* about so-called "rape rooms" inside startup offices and in the backs of high-end restaurants, we don't even want to be in those rooms.

I also encounter women who do not support other women. I say that these women left their "women cards" at the door. They ascribe to the philosophy that there's only room for one woman at the table and that they will do anything to get that seat. They tear down or throw out obstacles and hurdles to prevent other women from succeeding, or even entering the room to join the table.

SETTING THE STAGE FOR THE "MESH NETWORK"

I spent a year talking about and attempting to work through the details of my own venture fund and couldn't pull the trigger on it. I couldn't figure out why I was having trouble until I went to the Hera Venture Summit, a women-focused venture conference in San Diego, and saw women from around the world successfully investing and getting more women to invest. One of them was an experienced angel investor in Orange County, Xandra Laskowski, who is also a contributor to *Changing Tides*. She brings her wealthy friends together to teach them how to invest in startups rather than buy another piece of art or property or write a philanthropy check. She sources the deals and helps with the due diligence and final paperwork while the other women write the checks to the startups.

I realized that I didn't have to try to fit into the existing "bro culture" when I wasn't wanted there anyway. We women need to build our "mesh network" of like-minded investors from around the country and the world. This mesh network needs to activate the capital necessary to create a whole new financial ecosystem that actively supports and invests in products and services designed for us, and then deployed by and for us.

I am not alone. I have connected with some amazing women (and men) worldwide, who are interested in shaking up the current venture funding environment. I don't think it's because we can't play with the big boys that we want to take our toys into a different sandbox. It's because that sandbox has been left uncovered in the play yard for too long and is too dirty and polluted to play in anymore.

We have the opportunity to build an ecosystem that is cooperative in nature, where we can focus on doing well and doing good, and go for doubles and triples rather than trying to hit it out of the park. The average return for venture funds is 5 percent, which is pathetic. The current approach is not working for most VC funds and it is time to change the game.

Right now, I am focusing on investing in digital health, specifically in FemTech (women's health) and PediaTech (children's health) because the healthcare system was not designed for or by women. There is a major gap between what we need and want, and what is available to us. This lack of availability presents a huge financial opportunity: women control 85 percent of the household healthcare spending in the U.S. In 2016, 3.4 trillion was spent on healthcare nationwide and the amount is growing. Investing in this space is a win-win because most of the founders are female and they are targeting women. My favorite recent example of this is a speculum redesigned by women for gynecology exams, which would also include a completely redesigned gynecology visit. Can you imagine male investors getting excited about that? I can't.

"We women need to build our 'mesh network' of like-minded investors from around the country and the world."

Last year I left Sand Hill Angels after two and a half years during which I invested in seven startups and learned a great deal. I hadn't intended to, but it turned out that six of the seven startups I had invested in had female founders and/or leadership. I didn't even realize this until I was at a venture conference over the summer and did the math. I had not focused on female-led startups, but it turns out that the startups with female founders/leadership have products, services, and business models that resonate with my value set and investment thesis. I've doubled down on two, tripled down on three, and two haven't come back for more funding. I won't re-invest in the one with the solely male founding team – not because they are men, but because I don't think they will succeed.

During my time at Sand Hill Angels, I also spent time on the board and led a few committees. For the first eight months of 2017, as the board member responsible for deal sourcing, I saw between 250 and 500 startups per month either in person, via a pitch deck, or over the phone. In addition to my position as a board member, I also led the life sciences special interest group and actively reached out into the investor and startup communities. It was an amazing learning experience for which I am truly grateful.

Now it's time to move on and use what I've learned, use the connections I have made, and parlay them into something new. I haven't figured out exactly what this will look like, but it will be based on cooperation, support and the desire to make a lot of money investing in women and their ideas. This won't be philanthropy. Fortunately, I know I won't be doing it alone as many others share my desire to create a global "mesh network" to help these female founders and investors succeed together.

I interviewed Jillian Manus of Structure VC on my podcast *Piloting Your Life* and we talked about the need to create onramps for women to get into angel investing, including the opportunity to invest small amounts of money to diversify their portfolios and build up their risk tolerance. AngelList seems to be a great way to do this. If you are an experienced angel investor willing to share your deal flow, start syndicating on AngelList and encourage new, female angel investors to learn to invest through you. We need more female syndicate leaders and investors on AngelList.

If you qualify as an accredited investor but aren't sure where to start and want to make your own investing decisions (with some support), join my syndicate on AngelList (https://angel.co/terri-mead/syndicate) and/or send me an email at ClassBravoVentures@gmail.com. I'll share with you some resources and my deal flow.

Let's work together to invest in startups, make some money and change the world for the better.

Terri Mead is the managing partner of Class Bravo Ventures and president of Solutions2Projects, LLC, a consulting company that provides IT strategy, IT compliance and expert witness services in the life sciences space. She is an active angel investor, podcaster (Piloting Your Life), speaker, blogger, and regularly advises startups. She is passionate about leveling the playing field for women, people of color and LGBTQ+. In her spare time, Terri flies helicopters around the San Francisco Bay Area.

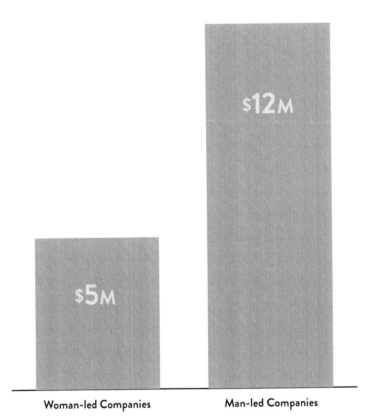

$12M

$5M

Woman-led Companies   Man-led Companies

Women receive less than half the funding in terms of deal size that men
do. For a woman-led company, the average VC investment in 2017
was a little over $5 million. For a man-led company,
the average deal was just under $12 million.

Source: Fortune
http://fortune.com/2018/01/31/female-founders-venture-capital-2017

Angel Investing: More Fun than Burning Cash in a Trashcan

By Xandra Laskowski

OSEA, Angel Investors

I WAS INTRODUCED to the concept of angel investing in 2013 and decided to channel some of my energy and funds into investing in a startup, as a way to broaden my family's portfolio. I was also interested in using my business expertise gained over the course of my career to help build more startups and start to change the direction of which companies are getting funded and therefore the decisions about which products and services are being brought to market.

When I speak to people interested in the world of investing in start-ups I explain to them that it's a risky venture. You need to think about angel investing as one of two options:

a)   either write a check for a (possibly) great opportunity or
b)   burn the cash in a trashcan.

When you are doing angel investing, it needs to be "play money," money that you could literally burn in a trashcan and it would not impact you or your family. The cold, hard fact is that the odds are stacked against even the most promising startup, so you need to be prepared for a loss at some point. Well, at every point, really.

So why did I become an angel investor if it's such a gamble? Because I want to be part of something that has the potential to succeed with my investment, that will give back to the community in the form of jobs and revenue, and possibly create more angel investors and hopefully more *women* angel investors.

The only way we are going to change the makeup of business top management and boards in this country is by empowering women to be a part of the conversation in making these decisions in the first place. When I first started to investigate angel investing, I participated in some traditional angel investments groups and realized that, since most of these groups had very few women members, the companies that presented their opportunities were in industries and sectors that appealed to the membership. This meant that the deals that received the most funding typically were male-lead companies.

I also know many women who are responsible for managing the family assets. I realized that, if I could create a safe space for them to learn more about angel investing, they might consider investing in startup companies instead of buying another home or piece of art. I saw angel investing as a form of financial activism and wanted to create a membership-based, private angel investment group focused on and driven by women executives and entrepreneurs with diverse and successful backgrounds.

"I saw angel investing as a form of financial activism and that is why I started OSEA Angel Investors in January 2017."

That is why I started OSEA Angel Investors in January 2017. This woman-focused private angel investment group inspires women to learn more about the angel investing world by offering education and access to early-stage companies looking for investors. We are very fortunate to be based out of The Cove, UCI Applied Innovation, which is the entrepreneurship center at the University of California, Irvine.

WHAT DRIVES MY INVESTMENT DECISIONS?

As an angel investor, several things drive my investment decisions. In the spirit of being honest and straightforward, I share these with you, with the hopes that they will help founders gain a better understanding of what may be going through the mind of your angel investor (which they may not share with you).

- *My timeframe for writing a check directly conflicts with when you need the money.*

Please understand, I don't need to write this check. As I mentioned, this is, and needs to be, play money for me. There is no urgency on my part.

The startup entrepreneur not only has to run and grow the company, but she has a time-sucking, soul-draining new role—chasing investors without being too intrusive or pushy as to turn them off from investing in her company. Well-advised founders know this and weigh the benefits of self-funding versus the need to fundraise.

- *I will write the smallest check possible.*

After doing the due diligence, I am ready to write a check, but I will invest the smallest amount allowed or possible. The way I see it, I can always invest more as the company grows its revenue and gains traction. And when I do decide to invest, I will come back to you with requests for things like term sheet changes and monthly KPIs. If I am investing with a large group or syndication, I will ask for a board seat. Expect those requests. Be prepared.

- *Founders and advisors must be investors.*

Why would an investor invest in a company when the founder has not? By providing the initial funding they have skin in the game and believe in the company's mission and potential. Advisors typically don't invest up front but are given equity for their advice. If an advisor does invest as well, this a good sign that the company is proving the model and moving in the right direction.

- *No one takes a salary until the company is in revenue.*

I have seen financial projections for startups that include large salaries before the company has money coming in. Before paying themselves anything, founders must obtain approval from the board and seed investors. It is important that salaries be below market and as minimal as possible to increase the chances that the runway capital will last until the company has some recurring revenue.

- *The CEO must be coachable.*

The company will fail if the CEO is not open and flexible and won't listen to advisors and to board input. For example, the CEO needs to know that at some point when the company is growing, s/he will be replaced. S/he may have been suitable to take the company from $0 to $5 million but now doesn't have the experience for the next phase. Investors and the board will want to replace the CEO with the right person to take the company to the next level. It is in the investor's best interest to protect their investment. The CEO needs to respect this and learn from the experience.

WHAT EVERY INVESTOR WANTS TO HEAR

As a startup entrepreneur, it is important to understand your investor audience. Get some mentorship before you launch your idea. Investors need to understand your value proposition. They will want to know:

- Why you?
- Why now?
- Why this company?

- Is there a market for your idea?
- Who needs it?
- What would they pay?
- What is the growth potential?

When you pitch to investors they will inevitably ask these questions, and they are looking for a reason *not* to write a check. Companies like Stitch Fix, Uqora, and Pending Parcel all found a white space that was not being served and built their companies to fill that need. Stitch Fix went public in November 2017 and Uqora and Pending Parcel are both proving their models with sales growth and attracting growth capital.

Startup entrepreneurs are my heroes. It takes passion, vision and lots of blood, sweat, and tears to build companies. Most entrepreneurs don't have a clue what they are taking on and that can be good too. As long as they are open to the right advice and have the passion to continue with their vision through challenges and setbacks, they have a fair shot at success. Knowing their own limitations and being willing to surround themselves with a team that fills in those gaps are vital.

I will end this chapter with one of my favorite quotes:

"We need to accept that we won't always make the right decisions, that we'll screw up royally sometimes – understanding that failure is not the opposite of success, it's part of success."

— Arianna Huffington

Xandra Laskowski is a startup consultant with more than 25 years of entrepreneurial experience with large multinational tech companies as well as with startups as a founder, investor, advisor and board member. She held positions such as worldwide commodity manager and national major accounts manager before moving into the angel investment and startup worlds. In 2017, she founded OSEA Angel Investors, a women-focused angel investment group in Newport Beach, CA. OSEA Angel Investors is an investment partner with UC Irvine Applied Innovation, Tech Coast Angels and Angel Syndication Network.

TOPIC	PROMOTION	PREVENTION
Customers	**Acquisition** "How do you want to acquire customers?"	**Retention** "How many daily and monthly active users do you have?"
Income Statement	**Sales** "How do you plan to monetize this?	**Margins** "How long will it take to break even?"
Market	**Size** "Do you think that your target market is growing?"	**Share** "Is it a defensible business wherein other people can't come into the space to take share?"
Projections	**Growth** "What major milestones are you targeting this year?"	**Stability** "How predictable are your future cash flows?"
Strategy	**Vision** "What's the brand vision?"	**Execution** "Are you planning to Turing test this?"
Management	**Entrepreneur** "Can you tell us a bit about yourself?"	**Team** "How much of this are you actually doing in-house?"

VCs ask promotion questions of men and prevention questions of women. Promotion questions focus on potential gains, whereas prevention questions focus on potential losses

Source: Courtesy of *Harvard Business Review*; See Kanze, Huang, Conley & Higgins, 2017, 2018.

It Takes a Village:
How Joining a Community and Increasing Your Radius Helps Female Founders Raise Venture Capital

By Suzanne Fletcher
Stanford StartX Fund

As an entrepreneur, the deck is stacked against you. As a female entrepreneur, the deck stacking is even more severe. Surveys find that up to 92 percent of all high-growth tech startups fail in the first three years.

A good way to increase your chances of success, especially as a female founder, is to build a support system by joining an entrepreneur community, whether a formal accelerator program or an informal network of founders. I know this because – as the manager of the Stanford-StartX Fund – I see it every day. Over the past seven years, we have supported more than 550 companies and our community is 1,200 founders strong.

Because of this experience, I know that a trusted community of fellow entrepreneurs can help you successfully raise venture capital. In addition to managing our co-investment style vehicle at StartX, I help founders navigate the process of connecting with investors and raising capital. For example, our fund will invest 10 percent of a round in companies that have come through the StartX accelerator, based on a set of objective criteria (including whether the founders want that investment). This is fully transparent and takes the uncertainty out of it for all parties.

Founders know how our process works, which alters the typical investor-founder relationship and allows us to discuss fundraising with true candor. It also allows us to be well-aligned with our companies throughout the fundraising process. They have the full support of a powerful community behind them to advise them and offer guidance on how to successfully raise the other 90 percent from outside investors.

USING DATA TO TRACK PROGRESS AND OUR IMPACT

My position gives me a birds-eye view of the industry. This allows me to share what I see, including some of the data that we've compiled, and tips that our founders use to increase their chances of success.

Within our model at StartX, we support founders of both genders from all types of industries and stages of investment and development. Roughly one third of our companies have a female founder. This is more than twice the industry average.

Trusted communities can support and benefit all founders, but I have seen a particularly powerful effect for founders from under-represented demographics (e.g., women, minorities) as they are able to connect with others and grow their networks.

During my time at StartX, I have seen female founders do extremely well. Here is some of the data:

- StartX female-led companies have a higher survival rate than their male-led counterparts. In our seven-year history, 91 percent of our female CEO companies are still operating or have been acquired, compared to 84 percent of male CEO companies.
- Our female-led companies are 40 percent more likely to raise Series A capital than the industry average (for all companies).
- Female-led companies that raise seed and Series A funding tend to gather more support from active angel investors, angel syndicate groups, and family offices. (VC dollars, on average, make up 10 percent less of a round for a female-led company than they do for male-led companies.)

Our data also tells us which VCs are backing more gender-diverse teams and which are not. This is valuable information we share with our founders—both men and women—when they are raising funds. Today, I am getting more and more questions from male founders, which underscores the shift going on in the industry right now. All of us can help get great companies, which more accurately reflect society, funded. This is not just a female problem.

"Trusted communities can support and benefit all founders, but I have seen a particularly powerful effect for founders from under-represented demographics (e.g., women, minorities) as they are able to connect with others and grow their networks."

CAN A COMMUNITY REALLY IMPACT FEMALE FOUNDER STATS?

We know the stats – women raise significantly less venture capital funding than men do. As a female entrepreneur, what can you do to increase your chances of success? In my experience working with over 100 female founders who have raised seed, Series A and Series B rounds, these are some tactical things you can do today:

We've all heard the adage that it takes a village to raise a child, the implication being that a community buttresses an individual, elevating her ability to achieve the ultimate goal of raising a child (or building a company in this analogy). The same is true for entrepreneurs. In my experience, I've found these three things to be true:

1. No person is born knowing how to run a company or how to raise venture capital. These are learned skills, and it takes a village to share and teach these skills.
2. Entrepreneurs are not "born into" a professional support system. It is something that successful entrepreneurs take the time to carefully

build and cultivate around themselves, often in the form of an entrepreneur community or accelerator-type program.

iii. Being a part of a strong community of founders can impact your
chances of success in a real way. Learning and getting constructive
feedback from knowledgeable and trusted people allow individual entrepreneurs to grow their skills and iterate more quickly and effectively.

TACTICAL TIP: SEEK OUT ROLE MODELS

If you can see it, you can do it.

I have noticed that when we host fundraising workshops, the speakers
and audience are predominantly male. It takes a psychological toll when
you are part of an under-represented group, whether you realize it or not.

As a female founder, it is important to picture yourself successful
and project that image to potential investors, employees and other business associates. We have found that hosting female-focused fundraising
workshops has a powerful effect—not because the messages or teachings
are different, but because seeing women on stage who have each raised
$50 million or more inspires and encourages other female founders to
ask for more.

My top tip: Connect with female founders who are one to two stages
ahead of where you are, and can be role models for you.

TACTICAL TIP: INCREASE YOUR VENTURE RADIUS

In speaking with and helping hundreds of founders, I've noticed what
I call the "venture radius" of founders definitely varies by gender. Ask
a 24-year-old male entrepreneur how many relevant VCs and angels he
already knows, and his answer is likely to be significantly higher than
that of a female entrepreneur of the same age. This difference in network

impacts the ability of female founders to raise capital at every stage.

We can speculate as to the reason:

- Is this an unfortunate by-product of the terrible behavior of some VCs in the industry?
- Is it because male founders' friends are more likely to become VCs?
- Is it because male founders have been exposed to a culture of investing in each other's companies in seed rounds? (Cap tables, which give a snapshot of the ownership structure of a business, show this is true.)
- Is it because the (mostly male) VCs tend to court male founders?
- Or is it a combination of the above, or a host of other reasons?

Regardless of the reasons for this initial disparity, women do have the ability to grow their networks to increase the number of relevant investors in their venture radius, and therefore positively improve their chances of success. A trusted community can help you navigate toward high-quality investors and away from the bad actors in this ecosystem.

Another important point about your venture radius is to start early. Don't wait until you are fundraising to increase your radius. Building relationships with investors is an integral part of being an entrepreneur. Investors and entrepreneurs should have a symbiotic relationship; each needs the other. Having more investors in your personal network is powerful, and allows you to:

- Build credibility
- Learn not to "pitch," but to have a conversation with investors and potential investors
- Gather important information about your industry and key metrics for raising the next round of financing. A VC may see more than 20 similar companies in your space. He or she can share what the annual recurring revenues (ARR) and other relevant metrics are to raise a Series A in your industry.

My top tip: Build out your venture radius – early.

TACTICAL TIP: PAY IT FORWARD

Successful entrepreneurs—both men and women—"hold the door open" behind them. This observation has been widely made by powerful women, who stress the importance of bringing people up alongside them, of helping junior colleagues. The same philosophy of support can be especially powerful when applied to female entrepreneurs.

So many of the female founders I work with are understandably so focused on the next stage ahead of them that they can't always see how many people at earlier stages are looking to them for inspiration. Paying it forward means helping women entrepreneurs at earlier stages get to know the investors and founders in your network. Coach them on their pitches; help them learn to successfully navigate an investor meeting; show them how to identify the right investors and how to build relationships. These skills will be invaluable for the women who come after you as they move forward through funding rounds.

Introducing other high-potential female founders to the investors you know also builds your credibility as a founder. Male founders do this regularly and women need to leverage this more as an incredible source of power. At the same time, the VC community needs to increase the number of female entrepreneurs they have access to. There are heartening signs of progress on this front.

Joining a trusted community will make it that much easier to find role models, increase your venture radius, and pay it forward. While communities and accelerators can benefit all founders, they can be particularly helpful to women and founders from other under-represented groups. By becoming a part of a community of peers, female founders can form bonds, share knowledge, and provide mentorship in a way that benefits everyone.

Our data shows that female founders who are a part of the StartX community have companies with higher survival rates than their male counterparts, and have especially high rates of making the leap from seed-funded endeavors to Series A-backed companies. As this data can often be overlooked or simply not tracked, my hope is more VCs will begin to think deeply about the business case for investing in female-led companies.

My top tip: Join a trusted community to learn ... and to mentor.

Special thanks to Cameron Teitelman, the founder of StartX who has taught me a tremendous amount about the psychology and best practices of fundraising; to Joseph Huang, the CEO of StartX who has been unwavering in his support of my efforts to do more programing directed explicitly at our female-founder population and lastly, to my favorite entrepreneur, my husband Mark Fletcher.

Suzanne Fletcher manages the Stanford StartX Fund, a co-investment fund run in partnership with Stanford University, Stanford Health Care and StartX. Suzanne's passion is working closely with entrepreneurs as they grow their companies. She oversees a portfolio of more than 300 companies, which gives her a detailed view of startup activity across many sectors and numerous relationships within the venture community. She leverages both for the benefit of her startup founders through fundraising advice and introductions to potential venture partners. She has a passion for increasing diversity in the industry. A Stanford M.B.A., Suzanne is happily married to an entrepreneur, and mom to human twins and lots of pets.

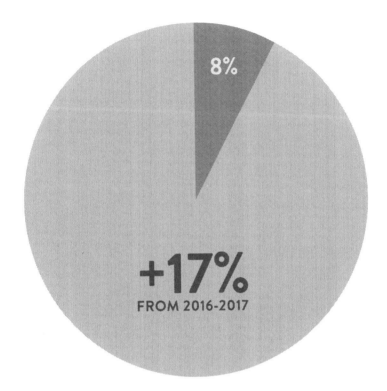

8%

+17%
FROM 2016-2017

**FEMALE PARTNERS IN THE TOP
100 VENTURES FIRMS**

There was a slight increase in the number of female partners in the top 100 ventures firms between 2017 and 2018. The percentage edged up from 7 percent to 8 percent in 2017, an increase of 17 percent. Another bright light in 2017: Eight firms in the top 100 added a female partner for the first time.

Source: TechCrunch 2017 Venture Report
https://techcrunch.com/2017/10/04/announcing-the-2017-
update-to-the-crunchbase-women-in-venture-report/

"What Did the Other Women Wear?"

By Amy Belt Raimundo

Kaiser Permanente Ventures

WHEN I WAS NEW to venture and just a senior associate, I attended my first board meeting as an unofficial observer. My mom's first question was "What did you wear?" followed by "What did the other women wear?" She was making sure I was appropriately dressed (at 32-years-old, mind you.)

Of course, the answer was that there weren't any other women at the board meeting. None on the board, none on the senior management team. Just me in my inappropriately formal black suit which was a carry-over from my corporate days.

I learned early on that women are still a rarity in board rooms and on executive management teams. I learned that you will most often be alone in that regard and will always stand out. I learned that your style, both physical and verbal, will be distinct. I learned that female stereotypes linked to weakness will be applied to you until you break them.

It's important to take your rightful place at the table and avoid the traps that undercut your points. Here are a few tips that can give you power when you are the only woman in the room:

- Speak definitively and knowledgeably.
- Exhale (don't inhale) while speaking so you are not swallowing your words.
- Strip your language of phrases such as "kind of," "sort of," and "just."
- End your sentences with periods, not question marks. This means end your sentences with a downward inflection, instead of the more typical upward inflection.
- Don't overly defer to your male colleagues or board members, because it will be read differently.
- Lower your voice slightly to command attention and focus.
- Take up physical space. Don't make yourself small while speaking or presenting.
- Wear your power clothes, whatever they are for you. There is no uniform for women in this world so find what gives you power. You will not blend in anyway. Wear clothes that make you feel great – it will affect your stance and how others perceive you.
- Interrupt as often as you are interrupted. Hold your ground if you haven't finished making your point.

"DEAR GENTLEMEN"

Years after attending my first board meeting, I attended my first board meeting as a member of the board. By that point, my mom had stopped asking questions about my fashion, thankfully.

I was again, the only woman in the room, and still relatively young by board standards. I generally felt good about my welcome and my contribution to the dialogue. That was until I received the follow-up email from the CEO.

"Dear Gentlemen" it began, addressed to the board. My first reaction was "Come on now. What is this old-timey thing?" In my 15-year career up to that point, it had never even occurred to me to address an email this way, but I realized that it was so commonplace in boardrooms that no one noticed.

Unfortunately, the next post-board-meeting email was addressed "Dear Gentleman ... and (oops! I forgot) Amy." This one was both more hilarious and more depressing. More hilarious because it underscored its old-timey nature. After all, it's a computer. He could have just deleted "Gentlemen" and replaced it with "Board" before he sent it. Was he also putting Wite-Out on the computer screen? It was more depressing because he was intentionally calling me out as the only woman in the boardroom.

What I learned from this was that, at best, men don't notice when women are absent. It's the norm. At worst, they make it known that a woman is present and single you out. This can be used against you as a tactic if you are not aligned with other board members.

How can we counteract this? Gender balance your board as much as you can. Keep that negative dynamic, particularly when it doesn't favor you, out of your boardroom. I've found women at the top beget more women at the top. Use your network to fill out the board including investors and independents. Just as men's networks are dominated by men; women's networks are dominated by women. The two companies I've been a part of who had female founders also had majority female boards.

IT'S ABOUT RETURN ON INVESTMENT

I had the opportunity to sit across from a large company CEO who was highly supportive of diversity and talked often about why having women at the executive levels mattered. His misconception, which I found common, was that women just liked to work with other women. My response was that I had always chosen to work in places where women were in senior executive positions not because I liked to work with other women, but because I wanted a good return on my investment.

It was a conscious calculation of my career trajectory. I didn't want to invest time and effort into a company from which I was only going to get cents on the dollar. Seeing women on the senior executive team was a sign that there wasn't some systemic bias in the organization that would inhibit my ability to advance in my career and reduce my return on investment.

What I learned from this interaction was that, despite studies that show that having a blended gender team (including boards) correlates with superior financial results, companies and firms don't internalize this. Instead, gender (and ethnic balance) gets filed under "the right thing to do" which never gets the kind of resources, focus and action that a "business problem" gets.

Systemic bias still exists within organizations but shows up more subtly. It shows up as having to prove yourself, sometimes multiple times, before getting the credit for your experience and insight that male counterparts with far less experience are given.

Getting promoted based on promise and potential can accelerate a career by years. Having to have "done the job" before you can get the job has the opposite effect. This also factors into investors' views of CEOs. First-time CEOs are always under more scrutiny, so adding another hurdle makes fundraising that much more challenging.

> "Target venture firms with female partners or who have consistently backed female CEOs. This helps to ensure that your experience and value won't be discounted."

It also shows up in the board room and can slow the progress of moving forward with an effective plan if the board demands greater and greater proof to support the approach.

So how can we get the return on investment that a diverse company will allow? Target venture firms with female partners or who have consistently backed female CEOs. This helps to ensure that your experience and value won't be discounted. Corporations are farther ahead than venture firms on this front and their corporate venture groups tend to reflect this. Review the leadership of the corporation and their venture firms for indications that you won't be discounted. You don't have time to waste in efforts that will only get you cents on the dollar.

EXPERIENCE MATTERS

I met one of my husband's old friends, a surgeon, while I was working for a medical device company. When I told her where I worked, the first thing she said was, "I love your product but the handle is too big." I was surprised at how top of mind it was for her and how clear her feedback was. When I reported that back to the division that makes the product, the response was that making the handle smaller had been on their product roadmap for several years.

The business context for this is that the number-one customers for the product were female physicians due to the specialty in which it's used. The other context provided by my physician friend was that the large handle meant she had to use two hands to close the device during surgery, which meant she needed an extra person in the OR to assist. So the dominant customer has a significant expense due to the product design but we hadn't fixed it (or designed it effectively in the first place). That seems like business 101 but it's not uncommon. When we can't appreciate the problem ourselves, we tend to dismiss it, even in the face of evidence.

This conversation reminded me that one thing that gives investors confidence in their decision to invest in inherently risky endeavors is a core belief that the problem has merit and therefore the solution has value. That belief is beyond the numbers and can often defy the numbers. It comes from experience, a "knowing" that no amount of diligence can create or undo.

Women are half the population but only 5 to 10 percent of investment partners so products and services that target them primarily have a "knowing" gap that is leaving significant money on the table. This is a problem for entrepreneurs and investors alike, not to mention the potential consumers who won't get the benefit of the technology.

How can you integrate this to ensure your product is understood by investors? If your product is meant for or bought by women, target female partners in venture firms. They are more likely to have this conviction around your product.

PLAY SHOULDER TO SHOULDER

As a recreational soccer player, now in a co-ed league, I've had some interesting experiences that serve as good analogies for the start-up and venture world. When two players are going for a ball, it's perfectly acceptable to use your body to move the opposing player off the ball, as long as there is no obvious shove. It's called "shoulder to shoulder."

As a 5-foot-3-inch woman in a co-ed league, it's easy to imagine losing that battle every time, particularly if you're unprepared for the contact. Befitting my "bulldog" nickname in high school, I instead use my low center of gravity and surprising strength to knock an unsuspecting player off the ball.

I've experienced the business version of this several times in my career. The venture and start-up world is a contact sport. You will meet resistance. You will likely get more resistance because you are a woman. You will be under more scrutiny. Rejection is common and validation is rare. I started my career wanting to be recognized for my efforts and tapped on the shoulder for key assignments and opportunities. I had to learn to ask for what I wanted and actively sell in order to get it. Sometimes this backfired and I got extreme resistance. That's okay. It doesn't have to go smoothly to be valuable and important. The more valuable something is, the more you have to fight for it. Someone else wants that ball, too.

What does soccer teach us about business? Don't be afraid of contact. Expect it, prepare for it and sometimes be ready to lower your shoulder if necessary.

DEVELOP YOUR OWN GOLF COURSE

In the middle of the financial crisis, I was sitting in the audience of a business conference. After the first two panels concluded and the third one took the stage, I started to seethe. As far as the eye could see, the panels were a "sea of navy blue blazers." All but 5 percent of the expert presenters were men.

It was a space I knew well so I knew that there were plenty of women experts in the field. They just weren't being asked to speak. This left the audience with the impression that women weren't experts and, in a world dominated by "pattern matching," this was a real problem. It also potentially indicated that the leaders didn't know who the women experts were. They were not in their networks so they didn't feel comfortable putting them on stage, sight unseen.

Networks are incredibly important in the start-up and venture worlds. Who you know determines who gets investment, board and leadership opportunities. When it comes time to invest, identify board members or syndicate partners, VCs reach out to people they know. Many of these networks are male dominated or exclusively male. This is often not by design, but is just the status quo. It started this way and propagates itself. Once networks get established, particularly when they take on a very male culture, it can be very difficult to break in.

So how can we change this tide? Create your own networks. As someone else aptly put it to me, "create your own golf course." Don't ignore, but also don't rely on existing networks that aren't designed for you. This disadvantage can be turned into an advantage by strategically targeting folks who are also underrepresented but highly valuable.

My reaction to the conference mentioned above was to create MedtechWomen, which harnessed the female experts and leaders I knew existed and were individually powerful but not getting tapped as often as they should. The organization consolidated that power by connecting those experts and leaders to create our own advantage to benefit the individuals and their organizations. We started as a single conference with capacity for 200 attendees, and in seven years have grown to sold-out annual conferences and 25 events nationwide, including events in cities such as San Francisco, Palo Alto, Minneapolis, Austin and Irvine. The "golf course" now includes over 2,500 "members".

WHEN OPPORTUNITY CALLS ... ANSWER

I was at another conference, this time in Chicago, about to leave my room for a business dinner when I got the call. "Amy, I have an opportunity for you." By the tone of voice, I knew the word "opportunity" had quotes around it.

The voice on the other end of the line was an executive at my company and a mentor of mine. The opportunity was the integration of a start-up we had recently acquired and the quotes were because it wasn't going well. This was not going to be easy. This could fail on my watch. But I took it anyway.

I took it because when your mentor and champion asks you to help solve a problem for them, you at least try. I'd like to say that I jumped in, made miracles happen to turn around the situation and it was a great success. I didn't; it wasn't.

After nine months of hard effort, collaboration and careful analysis, we shut down the program. But my willingness to solve an important problem mattered. My work, even in a losing effort, mattered. I got promoted and I learned a lot that continues to be valuable to me and my work today. This has been a recurrent theme in my career and in the success I see in others.

Through this experience, I learned that you can't just play by the playbook as your male counterparts and expect the same reward. You won't get as much credit, so you need to take more risks to keep your career on the same trajectory. Few women have come before you, but not for lack of trying or skill. Playing it safe and checking the boxes won't work.

The lessons learned from this somewhat painful experience?

- Step functions in careers happen in those moments. Partially because you step up to the occasion and people notice. Partially because you actually learn a ton that makes you better.
- You have to play a riskier game to win.
  - Take on the tough assignment
  - Develop a new, valuable expertise
  - Create your own organization
  - Jump between the seams of industries where few have gone but much opportunity lies

By sharing these stories, I hope to have given you some perspective on how to seize the opportunities when they arise, and how to handle yourself when you're under more scrutiny. Our differences as women can actually be an advantage, if we play our cards right. Half the world's population is not a niche but a powerful force. You can be successful in securing funding and developing a network of women who will enable your ambitions.

Amy Belt Raimundo is the managing director of Kaiser Permanente Ventures. Amy brings over 20 years of experience in healthcare investing, start-up and corporate operations and hospital system consulting, including as vice president at Covidien Ventures and Advanced Technology Ventures (ATV). Amy is a Kauffman Venture Fellow as well as the founder and president of MedtechWomen.

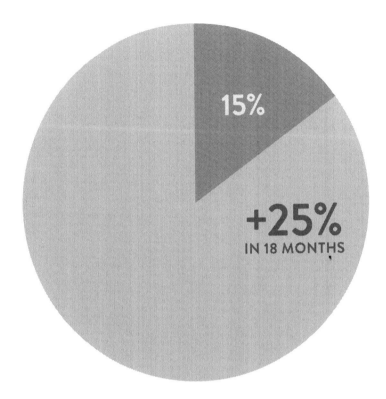

**FEMALE PARTNERS IN THE TOP
100 ACCELERATORS AND CORPORATE
VENTURES FIRMS**

Accelerators and corporate venture firms have seen the most movement
in bringing female partners into their ranks. As of 2017, 15% of
partner roles at accelerators and corporate venture firms are
held by women, up 25% in just 18 months.

Source: TechCrunch 2017 Venture Report
https://techcrunch.com/2017/10/04/announcing-the-2017-update-to-
the-crunchbase-women-in-venture-report/

The Strength of User Empathy

By Mokund Mohan

BuildDirect Technologies

IN THE THREE YEARS THAT I RAN MICROSOFT Ventures Accelerator programs in India and Seattle, I evaluated over 1,800 proposals, which resulted in 106 investments. I observed a unique strength that women entrepreneurs bring to the table. Women entrepreneurs have significantly higher user (customer) empathy, which resulted in early adopter retention rates 8 to 11 percent higher, and user churn 50 to 75 basis points lower, than that of their male counterparts.

These numbers bore out both on a cohort basis (women founders in a single cohort of investments compared to other founders in the same cohort), as well as on the aggregate (women founders overall across a portfolio of investments).

Since I am neither a behavioral scientist nor a trained psychologist, I am unable to explain why women entrepreneurs have more user empathy. I am simply sharing my observations for further exploration, and am highlighting a competitive strength that women should leverage during their interactions with investors.

If I try to identify the patterns among the women entrepreneurs I have worked with, there are three clearly recognizable traits tied to people with high user empathy. They are active observers; they are extremely resilient; and they are incredibly resourceful, which helps them iterate through problem-solution loops more quickly.

OBSERVATION

Most successful entrepreneurs I know have a heightened sense of observation. And I have noticed that women are significantly more alert than most men. They watch everything. I mean they observe at least 50 to 80 percent more than the average man. I learned this from Sharmili Ghosh, a successful entrepreneur who is the president of TIE Seattle (The Indus Entrepreneurs). She is one of the most astute observers I know and, as the first woman president of TIE, has taught me more about observation than anyone else.

Most people who are not entrepreneurs see the same things as an entrepreneur does; the difference is that they don't observe. I learned a technique called active observation from my mentor. It is seeing, then going a step further and asking questions about what you have seen. As you know, questions are at the root of solving problems.

To discipline yourself to constantly be actively observing, you need to train your mind to look, then ask, not to constantly keep looking or thinking. There is a downside to active observation: it is that you are not in the "present." Critics will point to the mind-rest that your brain needs, which helps it recuperate and rejuvenate. Some might also say that you should just go with the flow to generate great results. I much prefer active observation when I am thinking about problems.

RESILIENCY

The second trait female entrepreneurs share is that they are more resilient than their male counterparts. Sairee Chahal, the founder and CEO of Sheroes, is a great example of this. Sheroes is an online career destination for women. The community has access to high-growth career resources, mentorship and support. Sheroes engages with businesses to help them connect with female talent in the form of employees, partners, customers and business owners. Sairee is India's foremost women-at-work evangelist and earlier co-founded Fleximoms, which connects women seeking to enter or re-enter the workplace with job opportunities, information, and mentoring.

Sairee became aware of the need for flexible options for women when she became a mother. Unwilling to give up her fulfilling career, she realized that rigid work formats are hurdles that most working women face at some point in their lives. Her personal experience told her that a "one-size-fits-all solution" to women's needs would not work. Some needed more flexibility in the times or days that they work. Others were only looking for or needed part-time work. She interviewed several women in the same situation and found they faced similar challenges. That motivated her to start Sheroes, which has helped hundreds of thousands of women find flexible ways to keep themselves engaged at work, trained and resourceful.

"Women entrepreneurs have significantly higher user (customer) empathy, which resulted in early adopter retention rates 8 to 11 percent higher, and user churn 50 to 75 basis points lower, than that of their male counterparts."

When I think of resiliency, it's Sairee who comes to mind. Resilient people have a bias towards action and their action steps are immediate. Surprisingly, the ones that I respect the most rarely "sleep on it." In fact, a mini-setback really spurs them towards the exploration of multiple actions or options to solve the problem. This seemed counterintuitive to me at first, since the advice most people give is to "sleep on challenging situations," but I guess different types of people are wired differently.

Resilient folks display the maturity to understand that setbacks are normal. They realize that the path to success is littered with multiple mini-setbacks, so each of these mini-setbacks only convinces them that setbacks are not failures, but successes posing as an obstacle.

Resilient entrepreneurs have a "true north" that keeps them going. That true north is usually written down, not just in their heads or their minds. They tend to revisit the "true north" every so often, maybe once a month, once a week, or each time they encounter a mini-celebratory moment or a mini-setback.

Resilient women are always making a backup plan for the backup plan. It is almost as if they realize their first plan will not work out, so they always have a Plan B and sometimes a Plan C. Over the years, many have told me that their Plan A rarely materialized. They spend as much time coming up with Plan B as they do Plan A, which leads me to believe that the Plan B's take more time and effort, but are also the ones responsible for progress.

I have also found that resilient leaders tend to be more disciplined and set up small routines to build momentum. Building momentum by identifying smaller steps that display progress tends to help them bounce back from setbacks and creates a great culture in their teams.

RESOURCEFULNESS

The third strength that I have observed in women entrepreneurs is that they are incredibly resourceful. My best example of this is Tammy Bowers, the founder of Lionheart Innovations, a mobile coordination app that helps caregivers (parents, doctors, nurses, etc.) of children with chronic health conditions stay in sync. (Tammy is one of the contributors to *Changing Tides*.)

Tammy's experience with founding a startup was a personal one: her son has a chronic health condition. After many months of working to schedule and coordinate health organizations and other caregivers, Tammy turned to technology to improve the complexities of caregiving, and the Lionheart mobile app was launched.

A decade ago, Tammy would have talked to lots of potential customers, raised a small "friends-and-family" round, and then tried to get some marquee investors or advisors to be associated with the company — to provide social proof.

Now there are platforms like Indiegogo and Kickstarter. Tammy put together an early funding campaign to see if other parents were interested in the tool to keep their folks in the know. Word of mouth from the Indiegogo campaign also got her a lot of publicity among bloggers, media and news outlets.

For entrepreneurs in smaller cities, getting the attention of Silicon Valley angels or investors is difficult if not impossible. Many local investors are willing to help, but they lack the ability to validate the problem and the need, and tend to invest in "things they know very well" or "those things that generate revenues quickly."

Enter crowdfunding. If you think it's only for hardware and creative ideas, you need to take another hard look. Seven of the 10 companies in the accelerator program at Seattle raised money on these platforms. Some raised $50,000, others more than $350,000.

A successful crowdfunding campaign gives you three things:

1. Customer validation: People (real customers, largely early adopters) put their money where their mouths are. You're not just getting "likes on Facebook." They are ready to commit dollars to your program or idea.
2. Funding: If you invest a little money into your product, typically the crowdfunding dollars can help you do the initial manufacturing and shipping.
3. Social proof: I highly recommend you talk to a few "influencers" who can back your campaign on these platforms. This will help generate publicity, spread your message and increase the number of your backers.

In summary, observation, resilience and resourcefulness are three common traits I have observed in the women entrepreneurs who have heightened user empathy. This strength leads to clearly better startup outcomes in the early stages than those founded by entrepreneurs with less of a connection with their customers.

One way to use this information and put it into action is to answer most of your investor objections with the sentences "I don't know the right answer, but our users have told us ..." or "In observing our users we have learned ...". This shows that the starting point of your frame of reference is your customer, an empathetic point of view that can give female entrepreneurs a competitive advantage when seeking funding.

Mukund Mohan, CTO of Build Direct, has been an active investor in early-stage technology companies based in the Bay Area since 2001 and in India since 2008. Mukund has held positions as director of Microsoft Ventures, director of Engineering & Strategy at Microsoft, and senior director of Product Marketing at Hewlett Packard. He has invested in over 25 startups in Silicon Valley and India.

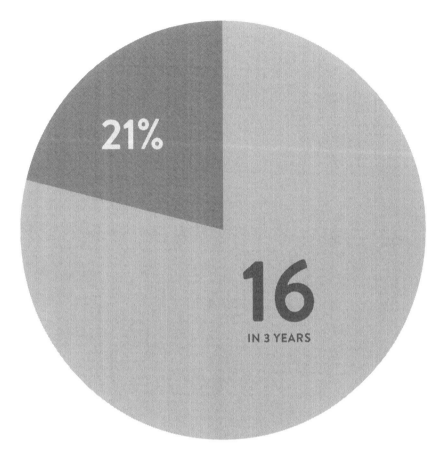

**WOMEN-FOUNDED VENTURE AND
MICRO-VENTURE FUNDS**

Another bright spot is the formation of new funds by women. As of 2017, 16 of the new venture and micro-venture funds formed in the last three years had at least one female founder, representing 21% of all firms in that category.

Source: TechCrunch 2017 Venture Report
https://techcrunch.com/2017/10/04/ announcing-the-2017-
update-to-the-crunchbase-women-in-venture-report/

How to Be Tenacious Yet Gracious While Raising Capital

By Deb Kilpatrick

Evidation Health

BEING A WOMAN CAN BE ONE of the biggest assets I have when fundraising in Silicon Valley. This is because that one factor immediately differentiates me from the vast majority of CEOs or founders that investors have talked to that day, week or even month. It's an advantage to be different in a market with so much available capital and so much company creation—both of which create noise around you and your message.

Because people so often remember a woman CEO simply because you "stick out in the crowd," it gives you a forum to get a meaningful message across about your company. It's incredibly important to be clear about what you and your company are really good at — and you cannot be good at everything, so self-awareness is key. Once you have clarified the unique value that personifies your company, whatever differentiates you can become associated with something special in a positive way.

It's important to be aware of the male-female relationship dynamics that can sometimes occur in the background of any given investor meeting, even when you aren't really conscious of it. This is particularly true for young women founders. Enter into funding conversations with your homework done; speak with authority; and make yourself seem as experienced as possible. It's especially important to remember that the first order of business in fundraising is to not get thrown by the "No." Hearing "no" is just part of the process; so view it as such.

> "Because people so often remember a woman CEO simply because you 'stick out in the crowd,' it gives you a forum to get a meaningful message across about your company."

Because part of the CEO's job is to find the right capital and the right fit in an investor, you also need to walk away from a deal that isn't right—i.e., you need to be able to say "no" as well as hear it. Remember that even the best companies with solid management teams can take a while to get funded, and every round takes longer to close than you expect. But any VC will tell you that she/he invests in people first and foremost. I think the best thing a CEO can do is focus on bringing together experienced teams and investors from really different backgrounds—and don't be afraid if it looks different.

THE IMPACT OF BEING A WOMAN IN SILICON VALLEY

"Evidation Health has the only board in Silicon Valley at the moment that does not include a white male as a voting member." That was once jokingly noted by the only male voting member (who is not white) who was on my board at the time. I think he may have been right, as surprising as that observation is in an area as diverse as Silicon Valley. I don't consciously think about this (being a woman) because I'm so used to it having been an engineering student in the 1980s, but I never forget I am different. I am extremely aware that when our female co-founder and I walk into a financing meeting, the VC might be wondering where the guy is. I counter this possible "background noise" by making it clear in the first few minutes that:

We're serious.

We're smart.

We're really good at what we do.

It can be frustrating, though, because this is inefficient, distracting, and wastes valuable time – both mine and the investors. The investors should be focused on assessing the skills of the management team, because they need to know who they are possibly investing in — as leaders, not as women.

Because my current company has an unusual number of women in leadership roles, I've been asked, "Why don't you hire more men?" My answer depends on who is asking the question. If I'm being asked by a (friendly) male VC, I can smile and respond with, "Why don't venture capital firms hire more women?" To him, I want to make the point that it's a complicated question, which has a complicated answer.

There are serious challenges to diversity in Silicon Valley technology companies, but these are complex things that have occurred over years and also relate to diversity in STEM education in the U.S. — so change won't happen overnight. I believe my generation of leaders has a responsibility to stop it from getting worse and work from there. Much like the recent wildfires in Northern California, the first step is to contain it. Sometimes we are blinded by not being able to totally solve something, when the questions we need to ask are "How can we change the trends?" and "How we can bend the curve in a new direction?"

MUSINGS ON MENTORING AND HOW MEDTECHWOMEN STARTED

My position on mentoring is simple: I believe strongly in giving back. I never paid any tuition for my engineering degrees (I received a B.S., an M.S., and a Ph.D. from Georgia Tech) and feel I've been given a special chance, and special responsibility, as a result of that. Mentoring women and people of color in STEM fields is one way of giving back, a tactic I can take where I often visibly see impact very quickly. I focus on offering guidance, mentoring, and advice that these people wouldn't necessarily get from others.

If we want to see a change and more diversity among leaders in Silicon Valley, women need to step up and actively create the next generation of leaders who are more diverse and who also appreciate the importance of diversity as a means of competitiveness. You can create sustainable change by doing your part and teaching others to do the same.

It's critical that we offer visual examples and verbal feedback to challenge perceptions and prejudices. This is partly why Amy Belt Raimundo and I created the MedtechVision conference and the MedtechWomen organization. We both realized that women experts were not appearing on panels or on the podium at the conferences we were attending, so we created our own forum spotlighting the world-class expertise of the many, many women in the medical device industry.

The annual MedtechVision conference gathers women leaders in medical technology to discuss industry issues in the face of key trends and challenges in the U.S. and global healthcare sectors. Our themes have included the empowered patient, new definitions of product "value" in healthcare, and sector evolution in the era of digital health. Our inaugural conference in 2011 has grown into an annual sell-out event in Menlo Park, California, with satellite events throughout the year in other U.S. cities.

THE SHIFT HAPPENING IN SILICON VALLEY

It does seem like the shift in Silicon Valley is accelerating around leadership diversity and the tides are changing. Four or five years ago, it became okay to talk about workplace diversity in the U.S. in general, and especially in Silicon Valley as related to tech companies and venture capital firms. Two to three years ago, people began to publicly acknowledge that there is a significant challenge with the degree of diversity in Silicon Valley, but there was no real consensus on what to do about it.

Now, over the last year or two there have been multiple lawsuits and high-profile cases in the U.S. related to issues around gender in the workplace. It seems that this has led to the conversation occurring across all circles and employee levels. I believe that the change in the consumer and personal parts of our lives can be a forcing function for change in the business and professional parts (i.e., it becomes harder and harder to have cognitive dissonance about what is acceptable—or not—in one arena but not in others). The diversity challenges in Silicon Valley are openly discussed now, at least way more than they were, and that is part of the significant steps being made in this arc of change.

ADVICE FOR WOMEN LEADERS

In closing, I offer some advice for women executives looking to raise capital and grow their businesses. To all the women I mentor, I try to get across three things:

You don't have to win every race. Some you just need to place, and in some cases, you just need to keep up.

Learn the difference between those races; stay focused on them; and don't burn yourself out.

Learn to turn your differences into strengths in whatever race you're running.

My favorite piece of advice for how to survive the sexism in Silicon Valley, or anywhere else, is that you must be tenacious but gracious. Focus all your energy on your goal. Don't let anyone distract you. If you are going to sit at the table, you must respectfully know your stuff when you get there. As my football coach father taught me—never, ever show up unprepared, because you might only get one chance to play.

> "The diversity challenges in Silicon Valley are openly discussed now, at least way more than they were, and that is part of the significant steps being made in this arc of change."

Finally, when I think back to what I wish I had known in my first management roles. It relates to being a better-functioning leader for the team. And there are a few other things I wish I had known earlier in my career, in the spirit of helping new leaders get a jump on their own development.

For this, I think it's critical to understand the difference between:
- Which situations to leave alone (i.e., when to observe and learn)
- And which ones need your immediate attention (i.e., when to decide and act).

Great leaders of great teams often have to learn to spend most of their time in the first category. Otherwise, you overreach in a way that truly hurts the team and other leaders' growth. For me, this is the hardest thing to do—but it is the single best way to build powerful, self-learning organizations.

 *Deborah Kilpatrick is the chief executive officer of Evidation Health. Prior to this role, she served as the chief commercial officer of the genomic diagnostics company CardioDx. Earlier in her career, Deborah held multiple leadership roles at Guidant Corporation, including research fellow, director of R&D, and director of new ventures in the Vascular Intervention Division. She chairs the Georgia Tech College of Engineering Advisory Board and is a Fellow of the American Institute of Medical and Biological Engineering. Deborah is a co-founder of the MedtechVision Conference, now held annually in Silicon Valley. She holds B.S., M.S and Ph.D. degrees in mechanical engineering with a bioengineering focus from Georgia Tech.*

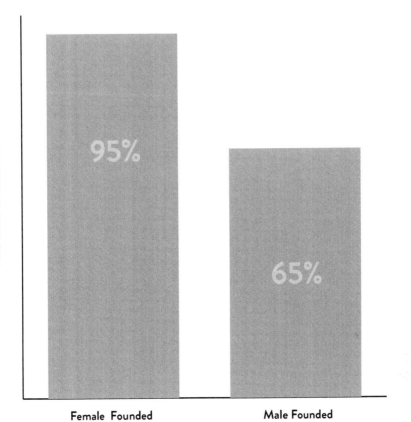

FINANCIAL TARGETS

95%

65%

Female Founded

Male Founded

Kevin O'Leary of the TV series, Shark Tank, sees better performance from female founders

Source: Inc. Magazine
https://www.inc.com/emily-canal/kevin-oleary-women-led-companies-shark-tank-inc-womens-summit.html

Going It Alone: Thoughts From a Solo Female Founder

By Dorin Rosenshine

Outleads

"WHAT DO YOU DO?"

For most people, that question is as simple as asking what they had for breakfast.

For me, it's a loaded inquiry. I know that I'll encounter an array of responses, from the uninformed ("You build websites and do SEO!" or "What kind of startup, in fashion?") to the pretentious ("You can't track me – I block my caller ID and delete all cookies!"*) and frightened or uneasy ("You advertisers are invading every aspect of our lives").

Most commonly, though, the response is enthusiastic, triggering a stream of questions over the next 15 minutes ("Did you raise money?" "Who are your clients?" "How many people work for you?" "Is there any-one else doing something similar?" "How does it work?" "When did you start it?" "All by yourself?").

It's generally fun to talk about my work, but there is too much of a good thing – especially when it's replayed over and over in a multitude of encounters and regularly overtakes the conversation.

To be fair, I can't really point fingers. Most people – those whom I'd neutrally label "mainstream society" – fancy the world of tech and start-ups, a sentiment that's been fueled by modern media and culture. A few years ago, I was one of them, yearning to invent a technology and enter the scene if only to be able to say that "I work at a startup."

---

* Both of these are irrelevant for our technology.

I've sobered up since then.

As a startup founder, it's my daily reality and, as you know, we quickly lose excitement over anything routine in our lives. It's basic human psychology, like how New Yorkers dash past Times Square while it's filled with awe-struck Chinese tourists. Meanwhile, the reverse scene is playing out in Shanghai.

To be clear, I still enjoy my work and hope to stay in tech for years to come. It's just that this journey has taught me a lot and in the process my perception has changed. The biggest lesson I have learned is that being a founder is hard – incredibly hard.

I realize how difficult it can be; so my goal here is to share some things that I wish I had known when I first started out. My experience is no magic bullet for success, but I do believe that having this information in advance would have made my journey a tad more bearable. This chapter is what I would tell my younger, less-experienced self, if I could go back in time.

Despite the help and advice from countless mentors, advisors, friends, and others that I have received over the years, I specifically chose to share the lessons I learned on my own, because I'm not sure that many of the mentors – the ones most often giving advice – are tuned in to some of the personal struggles experienced by entrepreneurs, and particularly female entrepreneurs.

Rather than reading like a dense textbook, I hope this imparts a friendly and conversational tone, sort of like you're talking to a friend over coffee. So grab a cup and let's dive in.

1. Have confidence and don't be afraid to upsell.

We know from studies and anecdotal evidence that, on average, women are much more risk-averse than men. Psychologists have proposed two reasons: (a) biologically, females have developed to be less comfortable with risk-taking, and (b) culturally, we're socialized to take less risks both in the way we are raised and by how society reacts to us (which is also learned).

This risk aversion makes female-led startups more likely to be successful because (surprise) thinking through actions before jumping in pays off. That said, several of the latest studies suggest that women tend to be so risk-averse that we're probably dismissing opportunities that have a decent chance of success, thereby leaving money on the table. This means that raising our risk threshold a bit will likely make us even more successful.

In my opinion, the biological tendency is a huge advantage that guards us against going overboard (unlike most men). It also makes an even stronger case for neutralizing the societal impact as much as possible. Whether you're raising money or recruiting, it's likely that you aren't being as forceful about your company as you should be. Given that, chances are that being stronger about promoting yourself, your skills and your company can help you achieve more without worrying about pushing too hard. Even though it may feel uncomfortable, don't undersell because, in the long run, that will feel worse.

As you're training yourself to be more "macho" – as society might call it – ask yourself: Where is mainstream society now? What is the current state in your relevant market? What are the default options or alternatives to your offering?

Remember (as any guy will tell you ...), it's not about your product being perfect. It just needs to be better than the competition. The first automobile would only travel a few miles before refueling; the first cellphone network supported only three simultaneous phone calls. My point: innovation happens in (often tiny) increments, and that's okay.

2. Starting a family and a startup are not mutually exclusive.

But it can be harder to do so later in life because, inevitably, kids bring additional responsibility. Physically, it's also easier to work crazy schedules when you're young, both because of age and because you're less likely to have a family and its associated responsibility.

Another reason to just go for it is that the importance of being first-to-market cannot be overstated. Whatever problem you're thinking about, chances are that other minds are trying to solve it as well – great minds often do think alike. Bottom line: if you have an idea, get on it today. In a few years, you'll be glad you did.

To you young and single readers: you can have a crazy work schedule and still have a social life. In other words: you'll still have plenty of time to party – I promise.

3. You can choose to be a solo female founder – but it's tough.

Really tough. If I had to illustrate how investors, clients, employees, and the general ecosystem judge a startup, I'd draw a quadrant graph with the horizontal and vertical axis representing gender and the number of founders, respectively (or vice versa, it doesn't really matter). Depending on how you draw it, each quadrant will represent one of four possible combinations:

GENDER	Male, Solo	Male, Team
	Female, Solo	Female, Team

NUMBER OF FOUNDERS

As much as I don't like to admit it, female founders are judged far more negatively than their male counterparts. Solo founders – male or female – are judged even more harshly. Investors worry that solo founders go solo because they don't get along with people, so building a strong team, which is critical to scaling the business, will be a challenge. To potential employees, solo founders are often interpreted as a symptom of a difficult personality. For clients, a solo founder company doesn't seem reliable. Typically, the general ecosystem sees a solo founder as an odd bird.

Even worse: being a solo-female founder places you in the most judged quadrant. In practice, that means that you will need to do a lot of explaining and your story needs to be extremely convincing to compel your audience. It's not impossible, just a difficult and frustrating exercise in mental toughness. If it doesn't kill you, it makes you stronger, right?

4. Focus on people who believe in true equality or, even better, are specifically enthusiastic about women's participation in tech.

It saddens me to admit it, but you'll face discrimination and harassment. It can happen at every situation where you interact with people, whether these are potential investors, mentors, or clients. Sometimes blatant, other times less so (if you have to constantly ask yourself whether you are being harassed, you probably are). Once you sense it – whether clearly or through your intuition – I believe that the best course of action is to ignore it and move on.

Even if you believe an investor, advisor or acquaintance has the top skills and connections that could turn your company into a unicorn next week, trying to work with people who don't take you seriously is akin to trying to build a relationship with the cute confirmed bachelor down the block (been there, done that). It won't develop into anything meaningful and you'll be wasting your most valuable resource: your time.

The sooner you eliminate these people from your life, the faster you'll be able to re-center your efforts on moving your company forward. Focus on the people who want to help you, and you'll go far. The best part? The fact that you've actually worked for your own success will make it that much more rewarding.

5. Prepare to be the only woman in the room – often.

This is particularly true if your startup is in the business of selling technology, even if it's a field with a decent proportion of women such as marketing (e.g., ad-tech). This is because higher-level positions – which are often the ones represented at conferences, seminars, and similar networking events – are still mostly held by males and also because tech events or workshops are often attended by people from multiple fields. So even if ad-tech were ever dominated by females, chances are that a tech workshop would still be attended by many men because the workshop might be geared towards ad-tech and gaming, for instance.

I've experienced a variety of scenarios where I was the only woman in the room; from a four-month incubator program surrounded by 40+ guys, to a conference lunch with 10 men, to a phone call with five male executives. The disparity is probably less acute now than it was when I first started out, but it's still blatantly noticeable.

My best advice is to simply have confidence. Remember that men, too, are people, and that one's hair, dress, or vocal pitch is irrelevant to the quality of one's offering.

It took time to adjust to my work environment being overcrowded with folks from the opposite gender, but once I did, I became far more comfortable around men in general, including in dating (a hidden bonus).

As long as you have validation and are further along today than you were one, three or six months ago, believe in yourself and your company, and project the confidence to carry the room.

6. If you can make it without investors and/or co-founders, do so.

You'll probably never hear this advice anywhere else because (in my opinion) most people with experience in an industry realize that making it completely on your own requires a mastery of mental strength that very few people are willing to sacrifice. Note my purposeful wording: I believe that everyone has in them the mental strength to succeed in that way, although most don't tap into it (and that's their choice). Heed this advice if you can; having investors and/or co-founders can make startup control and management far more complicated.

My first few years as a founder were excruciatingly difficult. Instead of pitching potential clients, I often found myself educating them on how to improve their online advertising. I pitched at many conferences and generated a ton of enthusiasm yet didn't land any sales. Most people thought my technology looked cool, but didn't really understand how to use it. I absorbed a lot of negative feedback from my mentors and advisors about not making financial progress, with one mentor even theorizing that I was simply seeking an ego boost from talking about something that nobody seemed to grasp.

About three years into my startup, I had lunch with a prominent expert in retargeting advertising – my startup's specific sub-field of online advertising. He had also started his own retargeting advertising company at around the same time as mine, though it ultimately drew him into a different sub-field of online advertising. He immediately understood my product and the underlying invention, then asked, "How are you doing with sales?" I mentioned that I was often finding myself teaching the technology, and he nodded. As it turned out, his company initially tried to market a solution similar to mine. In their efforts, they too encountered an overwhelming need for education, which delayed revenues. Pressure from investors ultimately forced him to pivot to another technology.

Luckily for this retargeting expert, he had a few other ideas and eventually focused on one of them. This wasn't the case for me. I had invested money to patent a specific technology early on and had built my business around that technology. It was all I had. I then realized that if I had raised money, I probably would have gone under quickly due to the burden of endless disputes with investors over the direction of the company.

> "I realized then if I had raised money, I probably would have gone under quickly due to the burden of endless disputes with investors over the direction of the company."

Similarly, working with the wrong co-founders can also quickly derail your success. Anyone with knowledge of the startup world – investors, employees, analysts – will recommend against splitting equity equally among founders. In fact, most investors will not write checks to companies that are equally owned, and many employees will not join them. Why? Because when disagreements arise, having equal ownership can result in a deadlock. This holds even if there are three founders, because the third individual might prefer not to take sides or even drop out. I personally know of several now-dissolved startups that could have survived if one of the co-founders had had more control than the others. Unfortunately, these scenarios are extremely common. Save yourself the headache and costs by going it alone, or at least maintaining the majority stake in your company.

Like everything else in life, starting a company has its advantages and drawbacks. That holds true whether you're going solo or with a team, raising money or bootstrapping, trying to introduce a new technology or to establish your independent business. Ultimately, the decision lies in your hands.

If you do decide to proceed down the startup road, I hope that the advice in this chapter helps illuminate your path. More than anything, endurance is key; entrepreneurship is really just a massive test of mental strength and, whatever the result, in the end, you'll emerge stronger with a one-of-a-kind experience to tell. I know I did.

Dorin Rosenshine is the founder & CEO of Outleads, a Microsoft Accelerator company. Outleads enables brands to engage customers with online advertising and relevant content based on offsite and offline data. Dorin has over a decade of experience in optimizing the digital presence for firms in a variety of industries, from consumer electronics to home improvement. Her work ranged from business identity to web application development, online ad budget management, and landing page optimization. A self-taught developer, designer, and copywriter, she has served as head of marketing as well as IT. Dorin lives in New York City and loves everything about it, particularly Central Park.

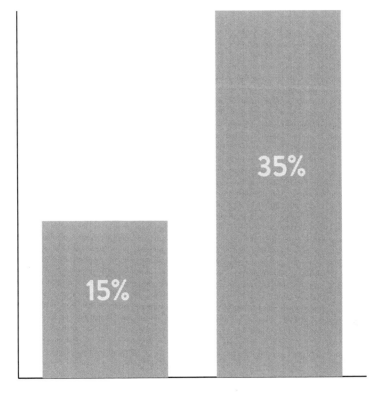

FINANCIAL RETURNS ABOVE NATIONAL MEDIANS

35%

15%

Gender Diversity

Racial and Ethnic Diversity

Gender diversity leads to stronger performance, providing financial returns 15% above the national medians.

Source: McKinsey & Company
https://www.mckinsey.com/business-functions/organization/
our-insights/why-diversity-matters

10 Rules I Live by as a Female Founder

by Tammy Bowers

Lionheart Innovations

WHO WOULD HAVE THOUGHT this is where I would be today? Five years ago, an idea came to me while I was caring for my son. I needed a better way to care for him and his medical needs. I thought, I'll start my own technology company. Why not? A stay-at-home mom with four young kids and no technology experience would be the perfect candidate for the rigors of starting a technology business.

As funny as it sounds, that is exactly what I did.

Although there were obstacles to overcome, as a mom solving my own problem I was the perfect one to start this business. I learned plenty of lessons along the way, some hard and some costly, but all part of the road.

RULE #1: HAVE PASSION AND FOCUS

Another entrepreneur advised me that he was starting 10 companies, knowing nine would fail, but one would succeed. No! That will not work.

If your company is to succeed you need focus and passion. There comes a point where you might need to stop and ask yourself ... are you truly passionate about this? Is this what you want to spend your days and your nights building? This passion might be the only thing that can get you through the tough times. This has probably been my greatest strength in this journey. I might lack other characteristics, but I am definitely passionate about what I am doing.

Passion can come from a variety of sources. My passion stemmed from somewhat of a selfish attitude, I wanted to build something that could help me better care for my son, make my life easier and make sure that I gave him the best chance at life. I have heard it many times (and I trust you have, too), the best ideas come from solving your own problems. No matter what you are doing, make sure you have passion that can pull you through the hard times. After all, it is the passion that inspires you to improve yourself, learn new skills, push through the hard times, and compensate for your weaknesses.

RULE #2: KNOW WHO YOU ARE AND WHAT YOU ARE BUILDING AND FIGHT FOR IT

When I was interviewing for a grant program. someone asked, "How can you be a CEO and a mom?"

As much as I want to think that the interviewer was not serious with this question, he waited in silence until I answered. I can be a CEO and mom, just like a man can be a CEO and a dad. It isn't easy, but as you always hear, anything worth doing isn't easy.

I was embarrassed at times for the lack of anything amazing on my resume. I finished college and then spent the last 10 years raising my family. When I told one of my mentors I was embarrassed that I didn't have anything that prepared me for running my own business, he stopped me before I could even finish to explain how everything I had done in the last decade had prepared me for what I was doing.

I thought about this and realized being a mom was the best possible way to prepare to be a CEO. On a daily basis as a mom I have had to manage multiple schedules, be in two places at once, be a nurse, taxi driver, counselor, and proficient in all studies including physics, chemistry, Spanish and even spelling.

10 Rules I Live by as a Female Founder

One of the biggest traits you learn as a mom is to put others first. You also learn patience and how to work with no sleep. There is no better training than negotiating with a three-year old or trying to understand what a two-year-old actually wants. I truly believe that being a mom has prepared me well for starting and managing my own company. When I was first starting this I talked to my family and my wise son told me "you are only guaranteed to fail, if you don't try."

RULE #3: KNOW WHAT YOU NEED

This is a big one. Especially when you are getting started, how do you know what you need? Starting a business and developing a product comes with a lot of unknowns and it truly is a learning process. A process in which, even to this day I continue to learn, especially as I make mistakes. I have split "know what you need" into two parts: product and people. These are the two essential hurdles for a company to be successful.

Product Needs

Before spending tons of time and money on product development, get as much feedback as you can. This was the focus of one of the grant programs I participated in. I don't know how many interviews, surveys and peer groups I held, but before I did anything I wanted to make sure that my solution would truly solve a problem.

Also I needed to make sure that someone would actually use the product, and that it didn't replace a problem with a new one. Even with the best preparation, you have to be flexible and even pivot if need be.

People Needs

This was something I have struggled with. I have been given so many amazing opportunities. Looking back what stands out are the mistakes I made by not making the most of these opportunities. I had people who wanted to help and wanted to see me succeed, but I didn't know what I needed and how they could help me. I had people who believed in me.

115

They too knew the pain of dealing with medical conditions and wanted to help, but I didn't know what I needed and how I could use their help.

During investor interviews, the investors often ask, "why do you need us?" They are looking for more than you just saying the money. They want to know why you want them as investors. What can they, personally, do for your company? This leads directly into Rule #4: build a team.

RULE #4: BUILD A TEAM

This might not be for everyone; you can do it on your own. (See Dorian Rosenshine's chapter "Going It Alone: Thoughts From a Solo Female Founder.") As much as I would love to say I did it on my own, I knew I could not do it alone. If I wanted Lionheart to be what I set out for it to be, I needed a team.

Now a team has meant something different at different points along the road. At the beginning of the journey my "team" was a set of advisors who helped me along the early stages, including helping me figure out even what I needed in a "team."

As I moved forward to becoming a technology company, I needed a tech co-founder. I have no technology expertise, and this was essential for my team. This is a bit of a debatable subject to most people. I got a lot of advice, especially from companies that wanted my business, who would tell me that I did not need a CTO, that they could act as a CTO. With thousands of dollars and months of time wasted, I learned a lesson. Again, it might work for you to do it on your own. Others advised me to learn to code and code the prototype myself. For me and my skill set, I knew I needed a tech co-founder.

More recently a team has meant investors who have the experience, knowledge and ability to build what I could not do on my own. Part of building a good team is Rule #1, knowing your strengths and weaknesses. If you don't know them in the beginning, this will become very apparent. You want to find people to fill your team who can make up for your weaknesses. Find someone who wants to be a part of what you are doing, not just someone who needs a job or can do what you need them to do. They, too, need passion about what you are doing. So now you know what you need, how do you find them?

RULE #5: ALWAYS BE NETWORKING

When I first started out I read an article about a new company that was making heart monitors for infants to help with SIDS. As a mom of a baby with a severe heart condition who had spent months watching heart monitors at the hospital, this company got my attention. The founders of this company were college kids from my alma mater. I used my new account on LinkedIn and sent a message to the CEO.

I have no idea what I was thinking or what I thought would come from the message, but I did it anyway. I told him how amazing I thought his product was and how much I wish I had had it when I finally brought my baby home. Then I told him my story of why I was starting my company and what I wanted to build. To my surprise, he wrote back. He gave me amazing advice and, above all, he gave me the encouragement I needed. He made introductions and gave me recommendations. To this day, I still turn to him for advice.

LinkedIn and other social networking channels are great assets today. You can use LinkedIn to find mutual contacts for someone you want to be introduced to. I use it to this day if I want to connect with another company. Relationships begin with one person reaching out to another. Use your network.

RULE #6: ALWAYS USE A VESTING SCHEDULE

Equity is valuable, sometimes it is the only thing you have to work with, so make sure you treat it like that. A vesting schedule has saved me more than I would like to admit. It is far too common for a founder or even one of the first key hires to leave the company. The problem with this, however, is if you have given them equity in the company and then they leave for any reason, they still have that equity and there is nothing the co-founders can do about it. This can be problematic when the product is nowhere near complete.

I am so grateful that I learned this lesson before I needed it, a few times. When founders, employees or even advisors are getting equity, make sure a vesting schedule is in place. Even the founders vest. I vested in my own company.

RULE #7: LOOK FOR PROGRAMS

When I came up with the idea to start my business the first person I turned to was my husband. From the beginning my husband has been my number-one supporter and it was his help that got me started. With his degree in business management, he introduced me to an amazing professor, a woman who ran the entrepreneurship center at his university. That was my first meeting with anyone about my idea. That one connection lead me to most of the turning points in my company. Through that meeting I learned about a grant program and my first accelerator. This same person also introduced me to my first investors and my first mentor. There are amazing opportunities out there, especially for minorities and women.

Grants

I have found that the best places to learn about these grants are the entrepreneurship programs at universities. I am well beyond my college years, and my degree has nothing to do with business or entrepreneurship. However, these university connections have been a great resource to me and to my company.

Startup Accelerators

These are highly competitive programs throughout the country. These programs build upon the startups' foundations to catapult them forward to investors and key influencers. I have completed two startup accelerators; they were the best thing I could ever have done. The training and connections I received through these programs are irreplaceable.

Pitch Competitions

Pitch competitions are a great way to make connections and also some startup money. They are highly competitive. However, they help you learn how to explain your company in a way everyone can understand.

These are just a few resources that I used. There is so much out there that can help you get that start you need.

RULE #8: FOCUS ON THE WHY

Find and focus on the story or the reason behind what you are doing. Rule #1 was about having passion for what you are doing. Rule #8 is about showing that passion to others.

One of the things I learned from the accelerators is to tell my story. Not just tell what I was making, but why I was making it. This is one of my strengths. I can list pages of weaknesses, but I have a definite strength in that I can tell my story and I can tell it in a way that everyone can relate to it.

Lionheart was built on the concept of finding a better way for me to care for my son, Landen "Lion" Bowers. In 2010, Lion was born with a large, failing heart. We were warned he would not live to his first birthday. When he was only three months old, Lion underwent a life-saving heart transplant, which resulted in a daily care schedule complicated by numerous medications and medical checkpoints. It was challenging to keep track of everything needed to keep his heart functioning properly. So I developed Lionheart to improve patients' ability to manage chronic health conditions.

As I tell the story people can feel the pain, even if they don't have experience with it. By doing this Lionheart is not just another company, but a company with a true purpose.

In one of my favorite Ted Talks, "How Great Leaders Inspire Action," Simon Sinek says you need to start with the "why." It is not "what you do" or "how you do it" it is "why you do it." People don't buy what you do; they buy why you do it. What you do is proof of what you believe. Inspire.

Another important concept is empathy, which isn't discussed much in business. It isn't about cuddles or being nice. It is about putting yourself in someone else's shoes. As Seth Godin says "People don't buy products. They buy relations, stories and magic." Find your "magic."

RULE #9: DON'T GIVE UP

No one will tell you this is an easy road. There will be ups and many downs. You will feel lonelier than you have ever felt. You will want to give up on a daily basis, sometimes multiple times a day. A wise friend once gave me a great piece of advice, "Every day tell yourself, I won't give up today, maybe tomorrow, but not today." Those are words I live by.

I once heard the quote, "if an entrepreneur's roots run deep enough, giving up is not worth considering." I think this is the key to not giving up. Make sure your roots are deep enough. Make sure you have the passion and commitment to make it through the hard days. They are bound to come, so be prepared for them.

> "You will want to give up on a daily basis, sometimes multiple times a day. A wise friend once gave me a great piece of advice, 'Every day tell yourself, I won't give up today, maybe tomorrow, but not today.'"

RULE #10: ALWAYS REMEMBER WHAT IS MOST IMPORTANT

This one is not as easy as it sounds and is sometimes the hardest. I remember one summer I just felt like I needed to get so much done that work became my whole focus. My family even went on vacation for a week and I stayed home to work.

My investor, who was also an advisor from the very beginning, told me to never miss a family vacation again. At the time, the work seemed like the most important thing, but the more I thought about it, the more I realized I needed better balance in my life. After all, I was building a company to better care for my son. My family should always be my first priority. If I put them first, kept my priorities straight, things would work out. The same with life. It might not always work out exactly how you want or in the timeframe you want, but it will always work out in the end.

 *Like many of us, Tammy Bowers was thrown into the caregiving world when her fourth child, Landen Lion, was born. He had a rare genetic disorder and needed a new heart. Tammy's life and mission were changed (for the better). When she needed a better way to care for her son she turned to technology and developed her own app, Lionheart, named after her son Lion. With the help and guidance of Microsoft, investors and mentors, she continues to build Lionheart. Her passions include her annual Courageous Kids Invitational track meet for special needs children in Utah, and also sharing better ways to use technology in personal healthcare. Tammy has been married to Joseph for 16 years. They have five children and live in Seattle, Washington. Tammy received her degree in child development from Brigham Young University.*

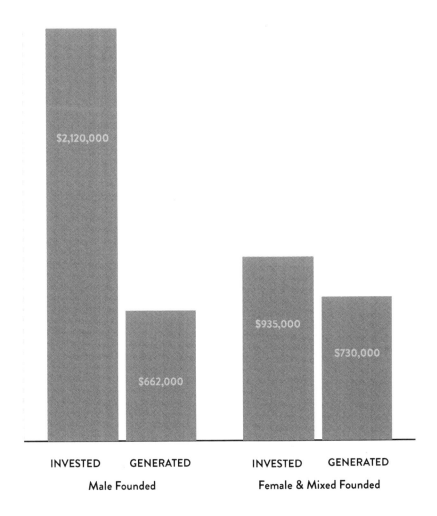

$2,120,000			
		$935,000	
			$730,000
	$662,000		
INVESTED	GENERATED	INVESTED	GENERATED
Male Founded		Female & Mixed Founded	

Women founders receive less funding than their male counterparts,
yet generate more revenue per dollar invested.

Source: Boston Consulting Group
https://www.bcg.com/en-us/publications/2018/
why-women-owned-startups-are-better-bet.aspx

Self-Care and Optimizing Yourself for Peak Performance

By Robyn Ward

FounderForward

WHEN I WAS IN MY LATE 20s, my friends staged an intervention. It wasn't for drinking or drugs. The intervention was about my work.

I was a founding team member of a startup in New York City at the time. It was my second startup and I had built a name for myself as the "Get-Shit-Done Girl." At the time, I was proud of this reputation. I was a triple Type A personality who would pull all-nighters frequently, and often be so focused on work that I would shut out my family and friends for weeks at a time. I was also eating three meals a day at my desk and making little time for exercise.

When my friends finally came together to speak to me about my work habits, I am ashamed to say, I didn't listen. After all, they didn't know the startup life and what it required. I told them they just didn't understand what it takes to build a successful business from the ground up. Instead of seeing their raw honesty and their attempts to truly help me, I shrugged them off, and plowed forward — always putting my startup before myself.

In fact, I went through several startups that same way: always on, always available, and always willing to sacrifice my personal life for my professional one. Then I switched to the investment side. From this perch, I watched as most of the founders I met with, and invested in, behaved the same way.

Ask any investor out there what her top reasons for investing in a startup are, and "strength of the founder or founding team" will make the list. Yet so many founders take in funding while simultaneously throwing their own health and well-being out the window. This is both counter-intuitive and counter-productive.

As a founder, your job is to bring your best self to work. You must walk into your office every morning as healthy, energetic, optimistic, creative, and productive as you can possibly be. Said another way, your job is to optimize you and your company, for peak performance. You simply cannot do this without prioritizing your health and well-being.

My own story, and my experience working on both sides of the table, is part of what inspired me to become a coach. I am passionate about helping founders scale themselves and their startups—and to do so in a healthy and sustainable way.

Founders, let me let you in on a little secret: No one is crushing it.

As much as we hear that catch phrase over and over again in the tech sector — *She's crushing it! They're crushing it! We're crushing it!* — the truth is that no one really is. Startups are hard and founders are not superhuman. It's not easy to start and grow a successful company, and there are many ups and downs along the way. Hence, startups are accurately compared to roller coasters. The fact that most of the tech world puts on a mask to make it seem as if everything is always going great adds to the pressure founders already feel to always be "*crushing it.*"

This type of verbiage and culture leads to even more stress and often results in the prioritization of company before self. The more realistic plan toward becoming the best leader you can possibly be — and to building the best company you can possibly build — involves prioritizing your own self-care. It's not optional. You must be intentional about what you need for your body, your mind, and your spirit, to not only be healthy and happy, but to perform at your peak.

Resilience is a much lauded trait in the tech world. And for good reason, but most folks don't quite get the definition correct. Resilience is largely about how we recharge, not just about how much we can endure. It's about breaks and rest and renewal, not about "toughing it out" or taking on the most pain or the most stress. It's about preparing yourself for the marathon, not for the sprint.

The need to take breaks within your day, week, and year comes down to biology. Something as simple as human circadian rhythms suggest to us that at some point (usually when it gets dark), the body and mind need a rest. Athletes know their bodies require recovery time. Founders should know that their brains require rest and recovery.

Research from the management consulting firm McKinsey & Company suggests that "always-on, multi-tasking work environments are killing productivity, dampening creativity, and making us unhappy." Their report also discussed the benefits of taking breaks to think about other parts of our lives (that part outside of work).

Unfortunately, employee burnout has become common in the United States. The psychological and physical problems of burned-out employees, which cost an estimated $125 billion to $190 billion a year in healthcare spending in the U.S., are just the most obvious impacts. The true cost to business can be far greater, thanks to low productivity and high employee turnover.

Some of the world's most successful people already know the price of cutting out self-care. They know all too well that burnout is not the price you pay for success, but rather that burnout can actually cost you success.

> "As a founder, your job is to bring your best self to work. You must walk into your office every morning as healthy, energetic, optimistic, creative, and productive as you possibly can be."

Media executive Arianna Huffington, who has become a well-known advocate for people getting more sleep, said, "It's our collective delusion that overwork and burnout are the price we must pay in order to succeed."

Ben Silberman, co-founder and CEO of Pinterest, brings the point home for founders: "Working all the time at the expense of your health and then cutting off all of your friends and family is probably not a good strategy because if you're actually going to go after something for a long time as an entrepreneur, having your health and your relationships intact turns out to be really important. And a lot of the folks who have burned out did so not because they ran out of money. They burnt out because they became socially isolated and really unhealthy."

SIX CORE COMPONENTS OF SELF-CARE

Through my own direct experiences, as well as observing hundreds of startups, I have come to believe wholeheartedly that healthy and happy founders build healthy and happy companies. It makes sense, right? The person in charge sets the tone and if you are bringing a great attitude, positivity, and energy to your people every day, they will feel that and mirror you. In fact, author and emotional intelligence expert Daniel Goleman says that: "50 to 70 percent of how employees view their organization's climate can be traced to one person: the leader. The CEO or founder at any organization creates the conditions that determine everyone else's ability to work well."

That said, it's important to recognize what self-care is and how to do it well. Self-care is *not* a "treat" we give ourselves once a month or once in a while (i.e., I'll let myself sleep in one morning this weekend or I'll schedule a spa day the end of this month). It's a daily practice that enables us to show up energized and engaged in our professional and personal lives. Self-care is, in fact, a habit. It's about your physical, emotional, spiritual, and social well-being.

Examine the following six concepts and think about how well you are doing at each one.

1. Sleep well.

Most people need seven to eight hours of sleep every night for optimal health and performance. Unfortunately, most founders I know get much less on a regular basis. Sleep deprivation leads to a lack of control, inattention, and low energy, all of which inevitably impact performance.

In her book, *The Sleep Revolution*, Arianna Huffington wrote, "We sacrifice sleep in the name of productivity, but ironically our loss of sleep, despite the extra hours we spend at work, adds up to 11 days of lost productivity per year, per worker."

2. Eat and drink well.

Food is energy, but not all food is created equal. Healthy eating leads to stable moods and energy levels, while eating sugar and junk food can cause mood swings and lethargy after the initial spike in energy.

Drink eight big glasses of water daily and keep your caffeine intake low. Startups, by nature, are cortisol-inducing environments. (Cortisol is the primary stress hormone.) Drinking lots of caffeine spikes your adrenaline and cortisol, which can be a recipe for heightened anxiety and stress, and shortened tempers. Pay attention to what you stock in your office kitchen. Opt for healthier snacks, foods and beverages for you and for your team. This makes everyone feel better and tells your whole team that you care about their overall health.

3. Move well.

As a general goal, for both your physical and mental health, aim for at least 30 minutes of physical activity every day. As weird as it sounds, in addition to positively impacting your mood, exercise is actually a cure for exhaustion. Many founders claim they simply don't have time for the gym. No problem. Walking to and from lunch and holding walking meetings are excellent ways to get your moderate exercise in. Plus, a Stanford research study found that creative output increases an average of 60 percent when walking.

4. Think well.

Many research studies have found that optimism and positive thinking lead to better stress management, better health and better overall performance.

Constantly reminding yourself of your "Why?" and visualizing the future state of your successful business are two ways to remain focused, energized and optimistic.

Another way to train your brain to think well is to keep a gratitude journal. Thousands of scientific studies have shown that developing a gratitude habit helps you feel happier and more optimistic.

5. Disconnect well.

Remember: Resilience is about how you recover, not how you endure. So build some times of silence into your day. It could be that five minutes with the door shut after a meeting is all you need to recharge. Strategic disconnecting restores the nervous system, helps sustain your energy and focus, conditions your mind to be more adaptive and responsive, and bolsters creativity.

Other ideas for disconnecting:

- Develop a meditation practice. I call this disconnecting through connecting to yourself and the present moment. Just five to ten minutes per day can make a difference.
- Commit to one disconnection day a week. I do "social-free Saturday."
- Take vacation time. Everyone needs time away, including the leader of a company. If you don't take a vacation, your employees will be wary of doing so.

6. Connect well.

As humans, we are a tribal species. Our emotions are contagious, and we rely on connections with other people for our own emotional stability. Make time to connect personally *(that means, in person)* with your friends, family, and loved ones. I also highly recommend joining a CEO group for support.

Also, schedule play time with your tribe. Many founders feel guilty about play, but shouldn't be. In addition, to making you happier, play time leads to greater adaptability and creativity.

You may think these concepts are simple and feel that intellectually you understand their value. The issue is that too many founders say: *I don't have the time.* However, it's not about having time, it's about *making* time. This is key — both to self-care and to many other important parts of life.

Making time for yourself and making time to figure out your needs are perhaps the best investments you can make in your life. Not just for leadership performance, but for your overall wellness and happiness.

Unfortunately, depression and anxiety are not uncommon in entrepreneurs. They're not talked about for fear of appearing weak. While I am certainly not saying self-care will eliminate mental illness, it has been proven to help manage it. Your mental health is just as important as your physical health, and it is important that, as an industry and society, we have an open dialogue about it. Under "connecting well," let's all add checking in on each other to the list. It's important to see how *we* are doing (not just how our companies are doing).

YOUR PEAK PERFORMANCE RECIPE

It's my experience that founders are so focused on planning for the needs of their business that they often completely overlook their own needs. To help, we have created a tool to guide you in evaluating your self-care routine and understanding what it takes to operate at your peak performance.

PEAK PERFORMANCE RECIPE	
How much sleep do I need?	7-8 hours a day
How much exercise do I need?	30 minutes x times / week
How much family time do I need?	
How much social time do I need?	
How much break time do I need ? (breaks in day, weekend time, vacation time)	
When I am at my BEST: CENTERED / ENGAGED / PRODUCTIVE	Disrupters from my BEST: EXHAUSTED / STRESSED / OVERWHELMED
Examples: meditating, eating clean	Examples: > 2 cups of coffee a day, skipping workouts
My optimal morning routine ("win the morning, win the day") is:	
My optimal evening routine is:	

Remember: success is a habit. Creating a strong morning routine is a big part of stepping into your high performance state. Be sure to list any components of your morning or evening routines that you feel contribute to being your best self, both at work and at home.

Keep in mind, there will be days and weeks in your startup journey where you don't nail your recipe. Don't beat yourself up about it. The goal is to be aware of what makes you perform at your best and to manage yourself for optimal performance over time.

MAKE SELF-CARE A COMPETITIVE ADVANTAGE

Optimizing your self-care is not just a "nice to do." It's a commitment to being the best leader (and person) you can be.

It's also a serious competitive advantage.

In fact, we encourage you to build self-care and wellness into your culture. Having your entire team taking great care of themselves and operating at or near peak performance will impact satisfaction, performance, and retention at an individual level. And, in the process, it will make your entire business more innovative and productive.

Once again, happy and healthy founders build happy and healthy companies. It's simple, but not easy.

Robyn Ward is a 20-year veteran of the technology startup space. She is currently CEO of FounderForward, a startup coaching and advisory firm. Prior to going out on her own, Robyn launched and ran the strategic investment fund at United Talent Agency. Before that, she served on early leadership teams at several venture-backed companies, including Docstoc, which was acquired by Intuit; and Verified Person, which was acquired by Sterling Talent Solutions. Robyn co-teaches a class on Venture Capital at her alma mater USC, where she serves on the Advisory Council of the Lloyd Greif Center for Entrepreneurial Studies. Robyn has been named a Top Woman in LA Tech by DigitalLA and a Top LA Tech Ambassador by TechWeek.

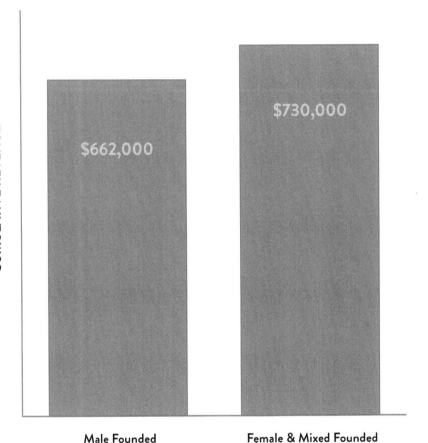

CUMULATIVE REVENUE

$662,000

$730,000

Male Founded

Female & Mixed Founded

Female-founded and mixed-gender founded companies
perform better than male-founded (comparative study of five companies,
based on an analysis of five years of investing and revenue data).

Source: Boston Consulting Group
https://www.bcg.com/en-us/publications/2018/
why-women-owned-startups-are-better-bet.aspx

What's Different about "Unicorns"[*]

By Jessica Livingston

Y Combinator

I'VE TALKED A LOT over the past few years about wanting there to be more women founders of the big winners, of the so-called unicorns. These are the founders who make the most influential role models, and role models are what we need most if we want to encourage more women to start their own companies.

In recent years there's been an increase in the number of women starting startups, and in the number who've raised significant seed and Series A rounds. This is good.

Now we've got to focus on the next target: more women-founded billion dollar companies. That is what I would like to examine in this chapter: what it takes to start a startup that's not merely successful, but massively successful.

I'm not saying everyone has to do this. You don't have to start a start-up. And if you do start one, you don't have to start a Google. But if you do want to start a Google, or think you might, what does it take? What's the difference between a successful startup, and a super-successful startup?

Fortunately I've seen enough of both types at close hand that I can see patterns of differences. I made a list of the things that I think are different about the unicorns, and there are nine of them.

---

[*] adapted from Jessica's talk from the Y Combinator 2017 Female Founders Conference

1. BE LUCKY

I want to get this one out of the way right from the start. In addition to everything else they need, the unicorns are lucky. One of the most important kinds of luck is timing. The most successful founders have the right idea at the right time. And you have less control over that than you might think, because the best ideas are not deliberate: they tend to grow organically out of the founders' lives.

However, while all the most successful founders are lucky, none are merely lucky. It is never a matter of having a great idea and then boom, a few years later you're a billionaire. Far, far from it.

2. HAVE THE RIGHT MOTIVES

One of the most noticeable differences between the founders of super successful and moderately successful startups is their motives. And in particular, the founders of super-successful startups are never in it mainly to get rich or to seem cool. They're always fanatically interested in what the company is doing.

Incidentally, it's perfectly fine to start a startup mainly for the money. But unless your motives change in the course of it, it probably won't wind up being a really big one.

There are multiple reasons why startups do better when the founders are truly interested in the idea. They work harder, since they love the work, and their enthusiasm is infectious. They think longer term. And they are much harder for another company to capture with an acquisition offer, because they don't actually want to quit.

3. HIT A BIG NEED

This one may sound obvious, but huge startups need huge markets. You have to make something a lot of people will pay for, or people will pay a lot for.

This is one place luck has a big effect, because market sizes are impossible to predict.

For example, the Airbnb founders didn't know how many people would want to stay in other people's homes. All they knew was that enough people would to make the idea worth working on. The founders of the most successful startups never realize, in the beginning, how big they're going to get.

So our advice at Y Combinator is not even to try to hit a big market early on. Since you can't predict these things, it's better just to work on something you yourself want, and then hope there will be lots more people like you.

4. DO SOMETHING BASIC

When you describe the biggest startups, most all of them are doing something very basic. Google is how you find information. Facebook is where your friends are. Uber drives you places. Airbnb gives you somewhere to sleep. These are all things you could explain in a few words to a five year old.

However, don't use this as a test for what to work on, because ideas often start out less general. At first Facebook wasn't where everyone's friends were; it was just where a couple thousand Harvard students were.

5. BE WILLING TO WORK ON A DUBIOUS IDEA

A site for a couple thousand students at one college doesn't sound like a very promising idea, does it? It may seem like a promising idea now, because we know how the story turned out, but it didn't at the time. Almost all the really big startups seem like dubious ideas at first. I know exactly how Airbnb's idea seemed at first, because I was one of the people whose job was to judge it, and I didn't think much of it at the time.

It's not just that these ideas don't seem as big at first as they later turn out to be. They seem to most people like bad ideas.

You need to be a certain kind of person to work on one of these bad ideas that turn out to be good. You need to be independent-minded. You can't care what other people think. It's now part of the conventional picture of a successful founder to be a maverick, and that part of the conventional picture is very accurate. I can't think of one that I'd describe as a conformist.

6. NOT BE AFRAID OF A BIG IDEA

You also need to be ambitious. Because what happens with these initially unpromising ideas is that they blossom into terrifyingly big ones. You start a site for college students, and pretty soon you realize you could expand to sign up the whole world if you wanted to.

At this point most people's reaction is fear. Signing up the whole world sounds like a lot of work. It also sounds like a valuable prize, and you have to fight to win those.

The fear of big ideas prevents most people from even realizing they could expand a site for college students into a site for the whole world. But a few people are more excited than afraid when this happens.

7. BE DRIVEN AND RESILIENT

Another thing I notice about the founders of the really huge startups is that I would not want to stand between them and something they wanted. All of them, 100 percent, have exceptional drive.

But, it's not always straightforward to tell how driven someone is. Drive can be suppressed when someone else has authority over you, like in most schools and jobs. In these situations, people who are really driven may even read as less promising than people who are merely obedient. So not only is it often hard for me to tell how driven someone is, people often can't even tell themselves.

You can tell after they start a startup though. No one has authority over you in a startup. Most people find that authority vacuum uncomfortable. But a few expand into it. A few think, "Ah, this is how life was meant to be."

8. FOCUS: LIFE'S WORK

Drive by itself isn't enough though. You have to be driven to work on this particular company. In all the really huge startups, the company is at least one founder's life's work. So they'd never willingly be acquired, for example. If you sell your life's work, then what are you supposed to do?

9. BE ABLE TO EVOLVE INTO A MANAGER

Early on, starting a startup is all about the product. But that changes when a startup gets really big. A founder who wants to keep running the company has to become a manager. You don't need to have management ability initially. There's plenty of empirical evidence to show that you can learn this on the job. But you do have to be able to learn it. You probably even have to like it.

Designing cool products and managing people are very different things. Most people who like building things dislike the idea of being a manager. It's a rare person who can be great at both. But you have to be to create one of the really big startups.

Those nine things, as far as I can tell, are the differences between startups that are merely successful and the ones that become really big.

But they're not just a list. When you put them all together, they make a story of how a "unicorn" happens. The founders work on something their own experience shows them the world needs. It wouldn't seem like a promising idea to most people, but they work on it anyway, partly because they understand the promise of the idea better, and partly

"The people on the path to being huge don't usually realize it, early on. But I'm hoping that if I can encourage just a few of you to keep going, then when you succeed, your example will encourage a wave of new women founders."

141

just because they think it's cool. As they work on the idea, they realize it could become even bigger than they thought. Instead of shrinking from that realization, they embrace it eagerly. This, they realize, is what they want to do with their lives. And they are so committed to the company that they're willing to morph themselves into whatever it needs.

There's a lot of variety in startups, but this is the most common path for the really big ones.

Remember, you don't have to start a startup, and if you do, it doesn't have to be a "unicorn." But if you do, this is probably what it will look like: an unpromising idea that blossoms into a frighteningly big one, and driven founders who see that opportunity and run with it.

I hope that some of you read this description and think, "Oh my God, it's like she's describing me!" The people on the path to being huge don't usually realize it, early on. But I'm hoping that if I can encourage just a few of you to keep going, then when you succeed, your example will encourage a wave of new women founders.

Yes, this is a very long-term plan.

But, after all, this is my life's work.

Jessica Livingston is a co-founder and partner at Y Combinator. She is also the organizer of Startup School, the big annual startup conference, the Female Founders Conference, and is the author of Founders at Work, a collection of interviews with successful startup founders.

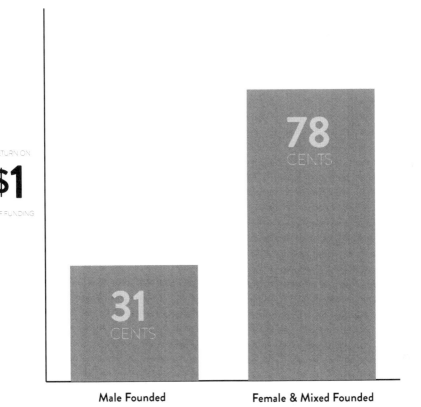

RETURN ON
$1
OF FUNDING

78
CENTS

31
CENTS

Male Founded   Female & Mixed Founded

Female founders generate more than twice the revenue
per investment dollar that male founders do.

Source: Boston Consulting Group
https://www.bcg.com/en-us/publications/2018/
why-women-owned-startups-are-better-bet.aspx

From Entrepreneur to Leader[*]

by Kate Purmal

Georgetown University Women's Leadership Institute

BECOME THE LEADER YOUR BUSINESS NEEDS

WE ALL KNOW that the caliber of the management team is a critical factor that determines, to a great extent, whether a startup gets funded … or not.

Between business inception and sustained success, many entrepreneurs take on leadership responsibilities. Founders become CEOs, COOs, or CTOs, often for the first time in their careers, and develop their leadership skills alongside the businesses they build. Often, startup leaders earn their place in the business due to domain expertise, not leadership experience.

There are five key skills to develop and hone as you transition from entrepreneur to executive leader. These skills are also critical to demonstrating to prospective investors that you are a strong and fundable entrepreneurial leader:

Decisiveness
Confident humility

---

[*] Adapted from *The Moonshot Effect* by Kate Purmal and Lisa Goldman with Ann Janzer

Resilience
Vision
Powerful communication

DECISIVENESS

Decision-making is often a challenge for founding teams that are relatively new to leadership. Inexperienced leaders struggle to know when to take charge and when to let others take the lead.

How do you make decisions?

A prominent Silicon Valley venture capitalist who listens to hundreds of startup pitches a year told us that he asks each startup team a simple question: "How do you make decisions?"

Some teams cannot answer the question. Others declare, "we decide everything by consensus." In either case, this VC sees warning signs of a startup team that might not execute well under the pressure as business dynamics change and the team grapples with rapid growth.

Consensus may sound ideal, but in the harsh reality of a startup, it can lead to delays and poor decisions. When everyone has input and every vote counts equally, decision-making takes too long. Worse, consensus often leads to mediocrity because it favors the decision everyone can agree on, which may not be the best course of action.

Agility is a startup's key advantage over established businesses. Ruling by consensus erodes this advantage, paralyzing decision-making. To pivot and react quickly, startups must be able to make decisions rapidly. The key is for a leader to remain humble and act with respect when making tough calls.

Gathering opinions and collaborating are vital. But decision authority ultimately needs to rest with someone. As you define the roles and responsibilities of the founding team, clearly delineate who owns each of the critical decisions, such as budget approval and establishing development priorities.

This shift can be difficult for the entrepreneur stepping into the CEO role for the first time. The founder of Judicata, Itai Gurari describes his experience as follows: "When we started, we wanted to be collaborative. My background in law and philosophy made me believe in the power of persuasion. I've come to realize that persuasion is not always possible. There are times I need to make the hard call and make a decision, whether or not everyone agrees."

RESILIENCE

The most important thing a startup founder can bring to the table isn't technical brilliance, a great idea, or sales prowess. It's resilience. Every startup endures setbacks and breakdowns. The successful ones survive and learn from these challenges.

The resilient entrepreneur regulates negative feedback and turns problems into learning opportunities. Setbacks ultimately develop strength, while mistakes and failure lead to growth. Resilience comes from within, with emotional resources and maturity. It develops with experience, which is why a startup failure can enhance an entrepreneur's value. You can actively cultivate resilience by adopting the right attitudes and practices from the start.

Adopt a Growth Mindset

The most successful first-time leaders are those who approach the experience as a learning opportunity. In her research into responses to failure, Professor Carol Dweck of Stanford University identifies a growth mindset as a critical factor to resilience and success. People with a growth mindset believe that they can change and grow through experience and practice. They see failures or struggles as an opportunity to learn. In the business world, the growth mindset translates into powerful leadership.

The leader with a growth mindset is open to coaching and feedback. He or she is not afraid of making mistakes, and asks for guidance.

"One of the key things I look for in a founder is their competence as a learner. Startup companies change at hyperbolic speed," says Sarah Tavel, general partner at Benchmark. "Founders and executives who don't possess a learning mindset get left behind by the company. Being a learner means you have the humility to be wrong. You can't learn unless you admit that you don't know something."

Build resilience into the culture

Entrepreneurs can build resilience into the business structure itself, making it safe for others to take risks. The Lean Startup methodology defined by Eric Ries, a Silicon Valley entrepreneur and author, entails iteratively testing assumptions and quickly learning from failures by making necessary adjustments. Treat the startup experience as a series of experiments. Some experiments will fail and others will succeed; that is the nature of experimentation. In an experimental context, every failure advances knowledge.

"A lot of successful startup companies seem like overnight successes. But behind every one is a founding team that has been working day in and day out, often for years," said Tavel. "What seems so easy from the outside requires an incredible amount of persistence and resilience. I call that grit, and that's what I look for in the teams I fund."

Manage Your Time

Stress and burnout are the enemies of resilience. In the early days of a startup, everyone occupies multiple roles. Startup founders often stretch far beyond their initial expertise. As the business grows, effective CEOs learn to protect their time and energy. An overstressed CEO is a liability to a startup.

Eager to keep things going, startup CEOs roll up their sleeves and dive into the work. They may spend time compensating for underperforming team members. Or perhaps they don't trust others around them enough to delegate tasks. Either way, important, long-term decisions and actions get sidetracked when the CEO is consumed by urgent, tactical activities.

Increase your resilience by being vigilant about how you spend your time and energy. If you're too busy to think strategically about the business and its course, ask yourself these questions:

Do I have the right people in place to manage and scale the critical parts of the business?

What am I spending my time on now that I could delegate if the right person were available?

What are the things that only I am equipped to do? Am I spending enough time on these activities? Am I leveraging my strengths?

Identify the areas and tasks that are consuming your time and can be handled by others with little training or oversight, and create a plan to offload those tasks. If you don't have the right people to take them on, start hiring. The most effective leaders are adept at identifying tasks suited for others. If internal resources aren't available, they work with consultants to clear the decks.

If you're worried about the expense of bringing more people on, evaluate the cost of not taking action. Ask yourself a fourth question about the current situation:

What would I contribute to the business if I could spend my time and energy on the things only I can do?

As the CEO of a growing business, you set the bar for resilience. Recognize that you are a crucial resource in the business. Your time is limited and precious. Preserve your time and energy for the tasks that require your attention and abilities, such as long-term planning, hiring, and strategic decisions, partnerships, and negotiations.

With the right people in place, a startup can operate more effectively and scale up more quickly. Recruit the right launch team and hire early and strategically.

CONFIDENT HUMILITY

Startups founded by groups of friends or colleagues often cherish egalitarian ideals. But as the business grows, someone has to step up to the role of CEO.

When you become that ultimate decision-maker, you're no longer one of the gang. Your words and behavior affect those around you and the very fabric of the business itself. Don't underestimate the impact of your leadership style on your team and the business. Whether you realize it or not, when you're at the top, you're always leading by example.

This advice isn't meant to make you feel powerful. If anything, it's meant to remind you of the magnitude of your responsibility. The best leaders for creative, innovative, and risk-taking environments practice confident humility.

> **Confidence:** Employees want visionary leaders who project confidence, make decisions, and promote the vision and the business. People will hesitate to take risks or innovate when they're not confident in their leader.

> **Humility:** Leaders in startup environments need to empower people to be creative to contribute to their fullest. The best leaders submerge their egos and listen to those around them, remaining open to advice and input, and sharing credit and success with others.

Lead Like a Hippo

With their team in place, a startup entrepreneur does well to emulate the hippopotamus; stay mostly underwater, with eyes peering above the surface, observing. Don't draw attention to your presence. Emerge when needed to make a decision.

An adaptive leader steps in when needed to break deadlocks or move things forward, trusting others to contribute and lead. The hippopotamus metaphor comes from a CEO who wants her employees to feel comfortable taking risks and trying things. She maintains her "underwater hippo" posture while her teams brainstorm and voice their opinions. She doesn't step up and take charge until there is a problem or until it is time to guide the discussion or make a decision.

If you have the right people in the right roles, and all are accountable for their areas of responsibility, then your role as a leader is to be present, observant, and supportive.

Adaptive leadership fills the power void, but leaves space for creativity and innovation. Effective brainstorming requires that people feel empowered to speak up and contribute to the discussion. This is the time to step back as a leader. When the team needs to tap your expertise or make a decision, step in to keep things moving.

Adaptive leadership flourishes when you have the right team in place and can trust the team to execute. This stance can be challenging for a first-time leader, but it pays dividends. A strong leader is adept at both stepping forward to lead and stepping back to share leadership.

"Truly perfect is becoming comfortable with your imperfections on the way to doing something remarkable."
—Seth Godin, author and marketing expert

VISION

"Entrepreneurs' inability to tell a compelling story may be the number-one barrier to success in getting venture funding."
—Lisa Suennen, Managing Director of GE Ventures

Vision plays a vital role for entrepreneurs or anyone pioneering a product category, an innovative device, or changed customer behavior. Visionary leaders steer teams toward unseen destinations as they develop and bring solutions to market.

In fact, demonstrating vision may be the most critical component of a successful startup pitch for funding. Lisa Suennen, a venture capitalist in Silicon Valley, published an opinion piece on why her firm invests their $557 million in less than .003 percent of the entrepreneurs who pitch them each year. She gives this advice to entrepreneurs: "Understand that the purpose of that first meeting is to hook us. Tell us a story. Make us understand through the use of specific details and imagery why the world can't really live without your product and why you are uniquely qualified to deliver value to the marketplace."

The better you define your vision for yourself and for your business, the better you will be able to collect evangelists, fans, and funders.

Jeff Hawkins, the founder of PalmPilot, invented the concept for the PalmPilot before today's smartphones and tablets. Like many innovators, Hawkins had a clear idea of what he wanted to create. He wanted his team to understand and share that personal vision as they developed the first PalmPilot, a handheld device unlike anything on the market at the time.

To make his vision come alive, he carved a balsa wood mock-up of his mental image of the PalmPilot and crafted the stylus from a bamboo chopstick. He carried this wooden prototype everywhere. He pulled it out during meetings, interacting with the block of wood much as customers would eventually use the real product.

Crazy? In Silicon Valley, startup entrepreneurs have permission to be a little crazy. But it was effective. Hawkins' wooden prototype guided the engineering team through key product decisions. It inspired everyone in the company to navigate the challenges and roadblocks they faced in developing this breakthrough technology.

Having a physical model clarified what was essential. The small screen area on the homemade prototype prevented the team from overburdening the design with extra features—the sin of "feature creep." It kept everyone focused on the ideal user experience. This story illustrates two key points: the critical role of vision in leadership, and the magnetic pull of a strong vision—even when it's made of wood.

Visionary Leadership

Who would you rather work for: someone adept at navigating politics and climbing the corporate ladder, or someone who inspires people with a bold vision and sense of purpose? Most of us would rather work for a visionary leader.

As part of their ongoing research into leadership, authors James Kouzes and Barry Posner have surveyed tens of thousands of people around the world about the characteristics they look for in colleagues and leaders. Honesty tops the list for both colleagues and leaders. But for leaders, vision ranks a close second. In contrast, only 27 percent look for vision in colleagues. Vision distinguishes leaders.

Visionary leadership is not exclusive to the upper ranks of management. People demonstrate vision by the way they lead projects or step up to take on challenges. Leadership can emerge organically at any level of the organization.

Perhaps you've taken the Myers-Briggs assessments. If so, chances are you didn't fall into one of the profiles associated with visionary leadership (INTJ and INFJ in Myers-Briggs terminology). According to the Myers-Briggs Foundation, these types represent 2.1 and 1.5 percent of the population, respectively.

A very small percentage of the population of the developed world fits the description of innate or natural visionaries. The rest of us don't think of ourselves as visionary.

What if we stop thinking of vision as an attribute that someone is born with, and instead realize that vision is a skill that we can cultivate and practice, like playing an instrument or swinging a golf club? From this perspective, visionary leaders are all around us, waiting to reveal their potential. Everyone can imagine the future. But few of us behave like natural visionaries and step into the future to experience those visions.

WOMEN AND VISION

A study by Professor Herminia Ibarra of INSEAD (a prestigious business school in France) compared evaluations of more than 2,800 executives across 10 different leadership traits. For nine of the 10 traits, women scored the same as or better than their male counterparts. The only trait in which women lagged men was envisioning—sensing opportunities and threats in the environment, setting strategic direction, and inspiring constituents. Although it may be a matter of perception, this lack stops women from getting to the top. Women who aspire to leadership will benefit greatly from developing envisioning skills.

You hit an unexpected patch of black ice while driving down the highway and feel the car go into a skid. Adrenaline rushing, what do you do? The experts offer simple advice for that situation—look where you want the car to go. When you focus on the desired direction, your instincts take over and you'll do the right thing to guide the car through the skid.

Envisioning in business works much the same way. Focus on where you want to go. See it in your mind's eye, feel it in your body, hear the sounds associated with its fulfillment, smell and taste it. A clear vision of the future guides actions and decisions in a way that isn't possible when you are immersed in the distractions of present reality.

A sharply defined vision pulls you forward toward your objective, leading you through treacherous stretches. It guides you through inevitable breakdowns, resistance, and problems along the way, both external and internal. To strengthen the pull of the vision, find ways to inhabit and experience your future goals as if they've already happened.

For example, if your personal goal is to climb the highest mountain in the world, go beyond visualizing the process of climbing and imagine the experience of standing at the top of Mount Everest. Imagine what you see, how you feel physically and emotionally, and who is present as you stand atop this peak. When you viscerally embody this future moment in your mind, the outcome becomes more real to you. Your neural circuits rehearse the situation, and it becomes part of your experience.

A similar thing happens when teams collaborate to create a shared vision of the future. As people create imagined experiences of the future after they have achieved their vision, they discover clues to successful future teamwork. A strong vision pulls people toward a future in which they operate with greater effect.

"Obstacles are those frightful things you see when you take your mind off your goals."

—Henry Ford

Travel to the Future

One way to get people on the same page for a future vision is to visualize, as a group, what will happen when you achieve success. Use the following exercise to close a planning session for your initiative.

Imagine that everyone on the team is together at the celebration after having successfully reached the goal. In this ideal future, acknowledge individuals on the team for their particular contributions to the team's success.

- Have everyone on the team take a moment to envision the celebration. Where is the party held? What does the venue look like? What sounds can they hear? What can they smell? How do they feel having accomplished so much?
- Next, ask everyone to hear themselves being acknowledged for their contributions to this future.
- Ask everyone to write down what they imagined: "I was acknowledged for _____."
- Share these glimpses into the future with each other.

This process illuminates how each member expects and intends to contribute. Something interesting often happens during the exercise—the team itself is transformed, linked by a common vision. Individuals understand their roles in the shared future and how to work effectively as part of the team. They discover the broader possibilities that emerge through the pursuit of their vision. This exercise creates strong, motivated teams that work together well as if they had already succeeded.

Make It Visible

When possible, create a visible reminder of the vision to inspire yourself and others. The wooden Palm Pilot prototype made a personal vision tangible for the entire team. Find your own equivalent.

One team imagined its project making the cover of a major industry magazine. A designer in the group quickly mocked up that potential future magazine cover and posted it on the wall of the dedicated moonshot conference room, reminding everyone of their shared vision.

The aspirational magazine cover works only when people spend time inhabiting the future vision. The visual aid is a reminder of a potential outcome that a team shares, not a way to prod people into committing to something they haven't yet experienced.

The pull of vision may be powerful, but it diminishes with time. Smart leaders refresh and sustain that vision, particularly when engaged on long-term initiatives.

In the world of business, the status quo exerts a strong gravitation pull. Inspiring people is only the start. Remain alert to opportunities to feed the vision over time, and keep your eyes on the future possibilities even when present difficulties loom.

"People often say motivation doesn't last. Well, neither does bathing—that's why we recommend it daily."

—Zig Ziglar

Powerful Communication

Securing funding and then gaining post-funding support from your investors requires consistent, effective communication. When you raise money, your leadership team accepts a significant risk. You owe it to board members, investors, and other advocates to update them with the information they need to sustain their support. The most effective leaders are adept at the art of managing up.

Too often, upward communications slide down the list of priorities. Communicating regularly and effectively with supporters and stakeholders is critical to increase your odds of long-term success.

Here are four reasons to invest time and energy in upward communications:

> **Ensure that contributions are recognized.** Give your team's accomplishments and your team leaders the visibility they deserve.
>
> **Stay on the radar.** Regular updates maintain the focus on your business and promote its success.

Turn supporters into advocates. Others have gone out on a limb to support your company. Give them information to champion successes, answer questions, and defend their positions. Any successes reflect positively on your supporters; provide information they can easily share.

Avoid surprises. If there's a potential problem, point it out and tell people what you're doing about it. Executives and boards of directors hate surprises. It's better to address potential problems and their solutions head-on than to lose trust when lenders learn of problems after the fact.

Cultivating the art of managing up brings personal benefits as well. Effective communication elevates your stature within an organization. The ability to distill and summarize important details and maintain a future focus separates a leader from a manager. To elevate your leadership, deliver concise, high-level communication framed in the context of future success and possibility.

How Communicating Up Is Different

When framing communications for your board of directors and high-level executives, consider how you can be effective given the unique constraints and realities of their roles.

Time constraints: Top-level executives and directors juggle unrelenting demands on their time. Securing a large chunk of time with a C-level executive or board of directors is nearly impossible. Be concise and plan for interruptions.

Linear vs. non-linear thinking: Many people in leadership positions are non-linear thinkers. They start with the big picture, then fill in the details, rather than progressing through points in a linear fashion to reach a conclusion. Match your communication to this thinking style.

Priorities and context: CEOs, boards, and investors operate within a broad business context. When speaking with the board or investors, understand their priorities and objectives. What looks huge to you may seem trivial to them.

Filter what you report to include only the most crucial information. The more senior people are, the less they want to deal with details.

Summary First, Details Upon Request

When updating people in high-level positions, communicate in a way that respects their perspectives and the demands on their time. Start by summarizing what your investor needs to know at that moment. Identify the essential takeaways, which may include potential problems or specific requests. Keep the details on standby and lead with the most important points.

This format applies to both written and spoken communications. For in-person meetings, spend time in advance identifying the important things you want to communicate. Ideally, keep the list to no more than three points.

For example, a status update to a board member might sound like this:

- "We're on target for meeting the July launch date." (The board member can relay this important status information to others.)
- "We're having a problem getting partner A to agree to our dates, but I expect to have it resolved in a week. If not, I'll let you know." (This heads-up about a potential issue prevents surprises down the road.)
- "I know Joan (another board member) is worried about the expense of this initiative. Here are three things I ask that you communicate to her to show your support and address her concerns." (If you have a specific request, make it clearly.)

Written communications follow the same format. If necessary, spend the time to draft a communication for this purpose, and have a colleague review it. It's a worthwhile investment.

Summarize so that others can focus on wins, specific requests, or proposed solutions to problems. If you think of the communication as a story, start with the ending and use it to build curiosity about the path that got you there. If you have piqued the person's interest, you may be asked about how you reached that point:

- "We found a way to double our new enrollments with a $10,000 investment."
- "The team has solved the customer issue and we're ready to meet the next milestone."

PUTTING IT ALL TOGETHER: SEVEN STEPS TO COMMUNICATING UP

1. **Be Concise and Lead with the Summary**
    Lead with a few key pieces of information the reader or listener needs to know. Drop into detail only when asked to do so. Whether you're talking to a CEO or a board, interruptions are common. Always start with three key points in case that's all you have time to cover.

2. **Speak Clearly and Plainly**
    Using industry jargon or vague terms distracts your listeners from the essential message because they'll waste brain cycles trying to decipher what you're saying. Translate arcane terms and details into relevant information.

3. **Be Relevant**
    What are the top concerns of your audience, whether it's the board, investors, CEOs, or other key influencers? Your board and investors may be focused on three to five top-level outcomes for the business

(growth, profitability, product-market fit, competition, etc.). If possible, reinforce how you are addressing these important priorities.

4. **Be Bold**

   Take a stand and make recommendations. If you see a potential problem, don't simply present the problem. Describe the steps you're taking to resolve it, or recommend a course of action.

5. **Be Specific in Requests**

   Decide in advance what you want as a result of the meeting and specifically ask for it.

6. **Reframe Results as Possibilities**

   Remind listeners about potential outcomes and possibilities of success. Keep renewing the inspiration that garnered support in the first place.

7. **Be Consistent**

   Make it clear that this is an ongoing communication. Let them know when they can expect to hear from you again. Find out how often they want to hear updates.

SCHEDULED REFLECTION

The busier we are, the less we tend to stop and think. Setting aside regular periods to craft upward communications is one way to build time for reflection into your schedule.

Research shows that taking time for reflection improves both productivity and learning. In a study of tech support call center trainees, people who spent 15 minutes each day reflecting on their training significantly outperformed those who spent the additional 15 minutes on more training. As you schedule time to craft communications for managing up, you benefit from the time spent in reflection.

For example:

- "I'll send another update in two weeks."
- "Once we hear from the partner next month, I'll let you know if we're still on schedule. "

Put the follow-up on your calendar. Earn ongoing trust by making commitments and sticking to them consistently.

Intentional and Regular Communication

Establish a process to maintain consistent upward communications.

- Who will receive updates? You might have multiple stakeholders.
- How often do they want updates?
- What's their preferred format? Do they need any special formats or types of information?
- What's the nature of their support (status, guidance, etc.)?

Use this information to create a plan for regular communications, as if creating an editorial calendar. Include these updates in your project calendar. Dedicate time and identify resources if you want assistance preparing data or graphics. Scheduling updates keeps important people informed, reduces micro-managing and frequent inbound requests for information, and prevents emergencies later on.

Use "So That" to Elevate Your Impact

Frame activities and contributions in the broader context of possibilities using the "so that" technique. Before you next communicate up, go through the following exercise:

- Make a list of results you have produced in the last month.
- Turn the results into broader accomplishments by adding "so that" or "which makes it possible to" at the end of each. For example:

- "After a lengthy negotiation, we signed the partnership agreement with Acme, which makes it possible for us to enter two new markets."
- "We solved the technical problem that delayed the beta, so that we can now ship. In doing so, we created quality-assurance and trouble-shooting techniques so that in the future we can spot problems much earlier in the development cycle."

Whether you're reporting the status, problems, or breakthroughs, future context gives advocates and others reasons to support your moonshot.

Speak with Authority

Pay close attention to your words when you speak to board members, executive teams, customer groups, and staff, both formally and informally. Speak in a way that others hear as leadership.

Start with the words themselves. Many people use filler words to buy time while they gather their thoughts. These verbal tics undermine authority. For example, the phrase "you know" impels the listener to provide support or affirmation, and thus saps the speaker's power. People in power can afford to pause. They hold the floor with intention and are willing to take the time to gather their thoughts.

Some words and phrases diminish the certainty of statements, effectively draining power. For example:

- "I only want to . . ."
- "It's just that . . ."
- "I'd like to . . ."
- "I think . . ."
- "It seems like . . ."
- "In my opinion . . ."

Ironically, adding the word "very" for emphasis often weakens the overall meaning. Consider the following three statements:

- "I'm very happy." – The "very" sounds like you're insisting too much.

- "I'm happy." – Simpler is stronger in this case.
- "I'm thrilled." – Better yet, choose a stronger adjective.

How you speak is almost as important as what you say. Vocal inflection can undermine the message of the words.

English language speakers in particular should beware of the practice of ending sentences with an upward lilt, as if their sentences are questions. This can sound as if you are questioning what you are saying, instead of speaking with authority. The only sure way to fix this pattern of "upspeak" is to notice it and intentionally practice speaking with a steady or descending inflection. Like a dedicated actor, pay attention to how you deliver your lines.

Speak Less

As you choose your words carefully, you may find yourself speaking less. Remaining silent works well for many leaders; when they do speak, their words carry more weight.

WORDS THAT DRAIN POWER

Here is a list of commonly used words that undermine power in written and spoken communication. Where possible, rephrase to avoid these words.

- Just
- Only
- Help
- Kind of/sort of
- Try
- But
- Should
- Need
- Think
- Seem

Many powerful CEOs attend meetings in near silence, carefully watching and listening, occasionally asking questions for clarification, but otherwise remaining silent.

When you choose not to speak you truly listen.

Silence allows you to hear and observe others around you, inevitably leading to better insight and leadership. Powerful silence may be particularly important for women in leadership positions. According to research by Victoria Brescoll, a psychology professor at Yale University, women in high positions who talk more than others around them are perceived as less competent than their male peers.

All leaders benefit when they prune unnecessary words from their speech, get to the point, and listen carefully.

Kate Purmal has spent her career in startups and thrives on the fast-paced, rapid-fire environment that characterizes these emerging companies. Kate relishes tackling the challenges that come with trying to unseat competitors and own markets, all under the time and money constraints typical of startups. Kate has sat in your seat and knows the challenges CEOs face. An accomplished C-level executive herself, Kate brings out the brilliance in the corporate executives and startup CEOs she advises. With her firm belief that most executives can become visionary leaders, Kate has mastered the art of inspiring executives and teams to accomplish the extraordinary while she holds their feet to the fire.

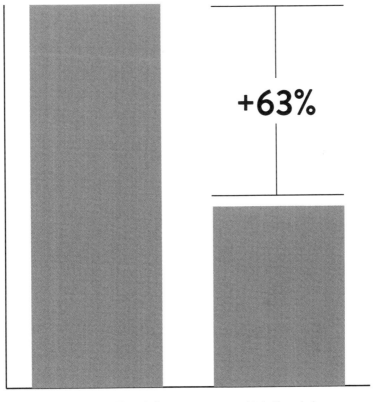

+63%

INVESTMENT PERFORMANCE

Female & Mixed Founded   Male Founded

Companies with a female founder performed 63% better than
our investments with all-male founding teams.

Source: First Round
http://10years.firstround.com/

Closing Thoughts
On Changing The Tides
By Debra Vernon
VLP Law Group

ON JULY 27, 2017, I sponsored a panel of women VCs at "The Pitch" event in Palo Alto, California. As venture partners Aileen Lee of Cowboy Ventures, Sara Deshpande of Maven Ventures, and Lauren Loktev of Collaborative Fund described their investment strategies, I felt like we were witnessing a historic shift in Silicon Valley's venture culture.

After the panel, I connected with Jennifer LeBlanc, who told me about her plans for this book. When she asked me to write a chapter, I was thrilled and said, "We all need to work together to change the tides." Jenn stopped in her tracks and responded, "That's the title of my book, *Changing Tides!*" It was a great moment – confirmation of our like-minded approach to strengthening the women's tech ecosystem.

Less than a week later, on August 2, 2017, *Fortune Magazine* published an article by Valentina Zarya entitled, "Venture Capital's Funding Gender Gap is Actually Getting Worse."

In the article, *Fortune* summarized a study of 2016 venture investment by data publisher PitchBook, which found that startups with all-male founder teams received $58.2 billion in venture funding in 2016, while startups with all-women teams received just $1.46 billion.

I crashed back to earth, deflated.

PitchBook's analysis of 2017 numbers showed little improvement. All-male teams received $66.9 billion, or 79 percent of the total $85 billion in venture funding, and all-women teams received just $1.9 billion of total VC funds. In 2017, women-led companies represented 4.4 percent of VC financings, a record since 2006. But the average deal size for women-led teams was $5 million while the average for all-male teams was $12 million. For example, PitchBook noted that the largest 2017 investment in a women-led team was $165 million (Moda Operandi), while the largest investment in a male-led team was $3 billion (WeWork).

Various theories are suggested for the gender divide in venture funding, such as:

- Men invest in founders from their social networks, and these networks consist mostly of men.
- Women are creating companies that don't interest male VCs.
- Men don't understand businesses that focus on women's interests, so they don't invest in them.
- Men invest in male founders because of a perceived difference in their commitment, bandwidth and potential.
- Women tend to raise rounds tailored to their company's actual needs, not outsized rounds that boost the numbers.
- The industry suffers from a lack of women VCs.
- We also suffer from a lack of women with STEM degrees founding tech companies.

Whether or not any of these reasons are valid, the numbers show little improvement.

WOMEN-LED BUSINESSES PERFORM BETTER

There is a solid business case for investing in women-led startups. Research by organizations such as Catalyst and the Small Business Administration shows that companies with gender diversity in their leadership and governance have higher profits. In 2015, First Round

Capital studied the performance of its portfolio companies from the prior 10 years and concluded that the female founders outperformed their male peers. Their investments in women-led companies performed 63 percent better than their investments in male-run companies.

Given these returns, what metrics are VCs using to pick investments? As *Bloomberg* reported in the May 2016 article "Who Gets Venture Capital Funding," VCs are most likely to fund companies started by male college dropouts (except for pharma and biotech startups whose founders are more likely to have doctorates). If being a male college dropout makes you a hero in venture capital, women can't win under the current playbook. We need a brand-new investment model. A model designed by and for both men and women. Where funding decisions are made in a process that is transparent and systematic. A change in the tides.

HOW TO CHANGE THE TIDES

I do not mean to imply that the entire field is flawed. Many investors already follow these tenets. They are trailblazers. Seek them out. Your investors will enter into a long-term relationship with your company. Diligence is key to the fundraising process. While investors do their due diligence on your company, do your own due diligence on your potential investors. Look for a good fit between your values and vision, and theirs.

> "You are needed in the room. This game takes grit and stamina. Arm yourself with a great team, supportive advisors and fierce champions and win it."

And female founders, by all means please do not quit. I've had quite a few Friday meetings with clients saying, "I will tell you Monday whether I am winding this down and getting out." I always say the same thing, "I will not let you quit." Founders, in those tough moments, know that you are not alone. Every author in this book and hundreds of other women will help. We mentor and advise, connect and promote. Do not be pressured, bullied or silenced. You are needed in the room. This game takes grit and stamina. Arm yourself with a great team, supportive advisors and fierce champions. Win it.

And it can be won. During 2017, the number of women-led companies in my client base significantly increased. My law practice focuses on tech startups, VC financings and acquisitions, so I see this as a sign of improvement in venture and tech.

The tide is changing but the pace of change is slow. Venture firms are naming more women partners, and more women are forming venture firms to invest in women-led startups. The stronger the women's startup ecosystem becomes, the more women will have successful exits, and the more women will have the power and capital to invest in women-led startups.

Technology can help accelerate changes in funding decisions through innovative ways to level the playing field. AI tools can help eliminate bias from the decision-making processes. Crowdfunding platforms are connecting women-led startups to a wider base of funding sources. In fact, the Crowdfunding Center analyzed campaign data from 2015 to 2016 that showed women-led campaigns reached their dollar targets more often than male-run companies. The analysis suggested that gender balance in the user base is key to this success.

Raising the consciousness of our own organizations will also help accelerate change. We can grow awareness by changing some of the ways we do business, such as:

- Making internal processes such as hiring, compensation and promotions transparent and systematic.
- Networking actively with other women.
- Directing opportunities to women-run businesses.
- Supporting the women already in our organizations, and hiring more.
- Nominating women for awards and recognition.
- Partnering with nonprofits that help women and girls.
- Becoming an angel investor in women-led startups.
- Collaborating with men who support women.

As I wrote this chapter, I thought more about the title of the book. I thought about what causes ocean tides – the gravitational pulls of the sun and the moon – and their traditional symbolism. In the art and literature of numerous cultures throughout history, the sun has represented power and governance and has been personified as male, while the moon has symbolized emotion, mystery and change, and has been personified as female.

These stereotypical associations sound dated. It would be nice if they were artifacts. But women confront these stereotypes daily in various forms. And we waste valuable time, energy and resources fighting so hard to rise above them. Imagine how much more men and women could achieve if we didn't have to deal with this century-old, epic, celestial gender tug of war.

The truth is that the tide-producing force of the moon's gravitational pull is more powerful than that of the sun. According to the National Oceanic and Atmospheric Administration (NOAA), it is about 2.5 times more powerful. Women can create a greater tidal force in the startup world as well. It can start in the tech industry. Innovation is what tech does best.

Debra Vernon is a partner in the corporate and securities group at VLP Law Group LLP, where she advises founders, companies and investors on issues faced by technology companies throughout their lifecycle, including formations, venture financings, mergers and acquisitions, and public offerings. Debra also mentors startups at the Nasdaq Entrepreneurial Center and serves as a founding director of The Athena Alliance, which focuses on increasing the number of women on corporate boards; and LabGirls STEM Initiative, which organizes events to foster girls' interest in science and technology. Debra began coding in elementary school, and received a B.A. in music and literature from Yale University and a J.D. from Stanford Law School. In 2016, Debra was a recipient of Silicon Valley Business Journal's "Women of Influence" award and was named in "Silicon Valley Women to Watch" by bizwomen.com.

Join the Community

Please join your peers online and continue the discussion at
JenniferSLeBlanc.com/ChangingTides

Ask questions
Post comments
Discuss ideas

JenniferSLeBlanc/ChangingTides

Or contact the author at
author@jennifersleblanc.com

About Jennifer S. LeBlanc

JENNIFER S. LEBLANC is the best-selling author of *Launching for Revenue: How to Launch Your Product, Service or Company for Maximum Growth* and curator of *Changing Tides: Powerful Strategies for Female Founders*. She is also the founder and president of ThinkResults Marketing, and owns the publishing house, HAL House. She is known as a high-energy and inspiring keynote speaker and workshop facilitator for startup accelerators and corporate teams. Her speaking and workshop events are designed to galvanize her audiences into action.

In her private coaching work, Jennifer works with female founders, entrepreneurs and change agents to provide them with the tools and connections they need to succeed. *Silicon Valley Business Journal* gave Jennifer its Silicon Valley Women of Influence Award in 2016, and ranked her company, ThinkResults, as the 10th Fastest Growing Private Company in Silicon Valley in 2017. Under her leadership, ThinkResults has also been recognized as one of the top Silicon Valley agencies (2013-2018). Jennifer has been an advisor to President Obama, Congress and the SBA via the National Women's Business Council.

For media, speaking, workshop or private coaching requests, please reach out to Jenn at author@jennifersleblanc.com.

Made in the USA
San Bernardino, CA
18 November 2018